David Hodgson

Letters from a
BOMBER PILOT

compiled from the letters of Pilot Officer J.R.A. Hodgson,
pilot in RAF Bomber Command, 1941–3

THAMES METHUEN . LONDON 1985

Acknowledgements

I would like to express my thanks to the many people who encouraged and helped me to write this book. In particular my brother Bill, whose knowledge of the history of Bomber Command was an invaluable source of information for me, and who, because of his closeness to Bob, was able to provide me with a vividly realistic portrait of him. In addition my sister Joan, my other brothers and sisters, and Mrs Bea Randall filled in many details of his life and of what it was like to be in this country during the early years of the Second World War.

I must also mention the kindness and help given to me when I was in Holland by Mrs Riny Palm, and also the researches carried out by Col. Arie de Jong, Leo Zwaaf, Gerry Zwanenburg and Major Willem Duyts of the Royal Netherlands Air Force. On the English side, the painstaking work of tracing what happened to the men mentioned in Bob's letters and of researching much of the background detail, was carried out with extraordinary dedication by my colleague, Jacqui French.

Finally, I should like to thank Catherine Freeman who commissioned the film that I have made in tandem with this book, and Nicholas Jones of Thames Television's Publications department for his support for this project.

David Hodgson

First published in Great Britain June 1985
Reprinted before publication 1985
by Thames Television International Ltd
149 Tottenham Court Road, London W1P 9LL

Distributed by Methuen (Associated Book Publishers)
11 New Fetter Lane, London EC4P 4EE

ISBN 0-423-01630-X -2

Cover design by Pamela Harris
Book design by Thames Television Publishing Department
Phototypeset by ✒ Tek-Art, Croydon
Printed in Great Britain by Whitstable Litho, Whitstable, Kent

Contents

	Acknowledgements	2
	Introduction	5
1	A Volunteer	10
2	Initial Training Wing	24
3	Learning to Fly	30
4	Operational Training	41
5	'Ditcher'	50
6	Wickenby, 12 Squadron	55
7	January 1943: Comedy and Tragedy	69
8	166 Squadron – Operational	76
9	Missing	83
10	1984: 22 May	87
	Index	96

To my wife Sheila,
and my children Louisa and Zoe

The Thames Television film of the same name, produced and directed by David Hodgson, was first transmitted on 18 June 1985.

Bob Hodgson

Introduction

On a warm clear day in the spring of 1978 my mother died. She was eighty-two, and had lain in Farnborough Hospital incurably ill for several weeks. Eventually she asked the doctors to stop the treatment that was keeping her alive. They gave her pain killers, and within a few days nature took its course. My father had died twelve years earlier, so my eldest sister Joan and my brother Bill were appointed executors of her estate. When they were sorting through her belongings they came across a bundle of letters in the bottom of her wardrobe. Dated between 1940 and 1943, they were correspondence between my brother Bob and my mother, father and a number of relations and friends.

Bob, my eldest brother, had volunteered as a pilot in 1941, and like so many young men had vanished one night over Europe. He had been flying with 166 Squadron from RAF Kirmington in Lincolnshire, and on 29 March 1943 an entry couched in the bleak phraseology of the time was recorded in the Operational Records Book: 'H and L failed to return, nothing being heard after take off.'

I was six and a half then, and as far as I was concerned that Bob was not there was nothing new. He had been away most of the time during the previous two years. On the day my family were notified that he was missing, I had cut my finger on a steel packing band that I had picked up in the street on the way home from school. I went into my house, tears streaming down my face, and was rather surprised to find everyone else crying as well. I asked what was wrong and was told, 'Bob's missing.' I doubt whether I really understood what this meant. I regarded him as my very tall, much older brother, who impressed me greatly by doing the Jitterbug with my sister in the front room of our house to Glen Miller's 'In the Mood', who peeled oranges with a knife, who made model aeroplanes, and who a few weeks before had given me a toy airman who walked if you placed him on a slope. This airman was called 'Dupe' after his Canadian bomb-aimer who often stayed with us. Bob once told me that on one of his bombing raids the flak was so hot that it toasted the sandwiches in his pocket. My childish brain was much taken with this incredible fact.

Bob making a model aircraft, with Bill and Leslie, in 1938

Of course my mother and father, and the brothers and sisters who were old enough to comprehend, were devastated. For the rest of her life, my mother would cry if the music of the Royal Air Force March was ever played on the radio. She always kept two framed photographs of him in uniform: one on the sideboard, and the other on the piano. This indelible sense of loss, of outrage at the events that conspired to cause his death, and of despair at the inevitable consequences of war, stayed with my mother for the rest of her life. It was an experience, shared by thousands of families everywhere.

Nearly forty years afterwards, for me, Bob was just a shadow memory. I had little idea what sort of person disappeared that night. None of the family knew exactly what had happened to him. He had crashed near Arnhem, and was buried next to two of his crew in a municipal cemetery just outside the city. That was about all that was known. I was therefore very curious when the letters that had been found in the wardrobe were given to me to sort out. I was surprised to find that, even after such a long time, reading the original letters conveyed so vividly the experience of being a young airman during that period of war. They described his initial training, the friends he made, learning to fly, booze-ups, crashes, falling in love, and going on operations. They were written with humour and honesty, and I consequently began to understand what he was like, and what he did.

I put the letters in order so that my children and the rest of the family could read them. The generation now growing up has no direct experience of war, and their secondhand view of it through many films and books bears little relation to the reality. Much has been written about our wartime heroes. Their stories have been told and they have been rightly honoured. But many young men were like Bob: they did what they were asked and died unacknowledged. Their deaths are recorded as the statistics of war, and it is easy to forget that the men who flew against Hitler's Germany were men of the highest calibre, chosen for their intelligence, courage, and personal qualities. Whether the best use was made of these attributes is another matter. The development of what has become known as 'The Strategic Air Offensive' as a military theory began in the 1920s and led directly to the manufacture of heavy bombers in the 1930s. The chief protagonist of this theory was Sir Hugh Trenchard, Chief of Air Staff from 1918 to 1930. He believed that bombers would play the decisive role in any future war, and although he had retired when the Second World War broke out, he was still an extremely influential figure. He was by then Viscount Trenchard, and his disciples commanded key posts in the RAF in 1941.

In researching the background to this period, I found a memorandum sent by Lord Trenchard to the War Cabinet in 1941. It contained his views on the necessity of increasing our long-range bomber forces in spite of the fact that we were suffering very heavy losses at the time: 'Such a policy may necessarily involve fairly heavy casualties, but the counting of such losses has nothing to do with the soundness of the plan once you accept the view that the nation can stand the casualties. The pilots in the last war stood it, and the pilots of this war are even better, and, I feel, would welcome a policy of this description. . . . It is quite possible to lose as many as 70% of your machines in a month, though these will not be all completely written off, as some can be repaired to fly again after crashes and accidents in England. . . . In the last war casualties of pilots were sometimes as high as 30% per month or more, but now owing to the universal use of parachutes, the percentage of those killed or wounded will be greatly reduced.'

I was incredulous when I read that memorandum. It seemed to me to be a wasteful and insular view of the resources of air power, based on ideas formed twenty years before, and out of touch with the realities of modern warfare. It received a mixed reaction from the

Chiefs of Staff, with the exception of Sir Charles Portal, the Chief of
Air Staff, who accepted Trenchard's main proposals on the need to
increase the long-range bomber force, but made no comment on the
likely casualties. Portal was particularly enthusiastic about
Trenchard's main thesis and wrote that 'the most vulnerable point in
the German Nation at war is the morale of her civil population under
air attack, and that until this morale has been broken it will not be
possible to launch an army on the mainland of Europe with any
prospect of success.' He added 'we can depend on the superior staying
power of our own people compared with the Germans.' Portal was in
fact advocating what was still considered to be barbarous by many
people — the bombing of areas of cities rather than precise targets.

I mention this particular exchange of views at a high military level
because they give an indication of the attitudes and military
philosophy of the Air chiefs. A vast amount has already been written
about the history of Bomber Command, and it is not my intention to
go over this ground again. However, when reading my brother's
letters I felt it was essential not only to seek out the details of his short
career in the Air Force, but also to understand the historical
background that led to the order to take off that night. Bob's life, and
the use that was made of his particular attributes in the national
interest, should be seen in the context of events and the decisions of
those whose job it was to take the responsibility of leadership. He was
one of over 55,000 airmen who were killed while serving in Bomber
Command. Their casualty rate was higher than any other British
servicemen had to face. The officially calculated average life of a
heavy bomber in terms of its replacement was fourteen operations.
The aircrews were expected to fly thirty. It is a tribute to the courage
of these men that they still went on flying, knowing the risks they
were taking.

I would prefer my children to remember not only the bravery of
the men who died, but also to understand that the loss of each of them
was a catastrophic event for their families. It is often forgotten that
for the most part the men who flew in Bomber Command were very
young — in their late teens and early twenties. The loss, therefore,
was heightened by a sense of the dreadful waste of young lives, of
much-loved sons coming to their maturity only to be destroyed before
their proper time. The statistics, the military thinking that sees all of
them as expendable units in a war, and the anaesthetic of passing time
all tend to obscure the real tragedy. The significance of Bob
Hodgson's story is that he was unique, just like each one of the others

who died.

Extracts from Bob's letters were used as the basis of a television documentary, and it was necessary to combine them here and there, to make a coherent narrative. They were never intended for publication, and by treating them in this way I think they convey more clearly what he thought and felt. When I embarked on this project I was also given further letters and photographs by other members of my family, and in addition I recorded a number of interviews with them, and with other people who knew him at the time.

I am adopting the same methods for this book, but of course the substance is far more detailed and comprehensive than is possible in a one-hour film. I hope it gives some idea of what it was like not just for Bob, but for all those young men whose lives were lost, and of what the loss meant to their families.

			SECRET.	
Wt. 39634104 10584. 3141 P.2 Ltd. 11—491				
R.A.F. Form 540		OPERATIONS RECORD ·BOOK	Page No. 3	
See instructions for use of this form in K.R. and A.C.I., para. 2349, and War Manual, Pt. II., chapter XX., and notes in R.A.F. Pocket Book.		of (Unit or Formation) 166 Squadron, No.1 Group	No. of pages used for day	

Place	Date	Time	Summary of Events	References to Appendices
Kirmington	29.3.43		**166 Squadron Operations.** Of twelve aircraft which took off to attack the target of ·OCHUM nine successfully located it and dropped 44 x 500lb. G.P. bombs; 1500 x 41b. incendiaries; 120 x 41b. X incendiaries and 136 x 301b. incendia/ries. "V" abandoned the mission as the captain considered the weather too bad at base area. Weather conditions at base were bad at time of take-off, but weather over the target area was good. "D" was attacked by a ME.109 and damaged. Other enemy aircraft were sighted and moderate heavy flak was encountered. Searchlights were active. "H" and "L" failed to return, nothing being heard from them after taking off from base. This was quite a successful raid in the face of stiff enemy opposition.	APPENdix A). Form 541
			Wing Commander, Commanding, No.166 Squadron, · R.A.F.	

Chapter One
A Volunteer

From the start of the war in September 1939, until August 1940, the Germans did not carry out any bombing raids on London. Most people living in the metropolis went about their lives normally, without the war causing any direct alarm. All my family were living at our home in Sydenham, in South East London. Bob, who was nineteen years old, worked in a film laboratory in the West End of London. He expected to be called up for military service, and wanted to join the RAF. He had always been fascinated by flying. It exercised a romantic appeal over the minds of many young people brought up in the period between the Wars that is difficult to imagine today. With my brothers Bill and Les, who were a couple of years younger, Bob liked nothing better than to go to Croydon Airport on a Saturday afternoon to watch the planes taking off and landing. Bill and Les were still at school, and in the hot summer weather of 1940 were away at a camp in Wiltshire. While they were there, they received a letter from Bob.

37 Woodbastwick Road,
Lower Sydenham,
S.E.26.
17.8.40

Dear Bill & Les,

Thanks for the letter, I enjoyed it very much. Just as I was finishing reading it on Thursday evening and wondering what I would write to you about I heard a faint 'grumble' of aeroplane motors. I took no notice however and went upstairs to Mum's bedroom to get a clean collar.

While up there I looked in the direction of Croydon (force of habit) and beheld a dozen machines dropping out of the haze. I thought they were British until I saw d. . . . . . great bombs drop from the first one. I let out a yell which brought the family up, and for ten minutes we watched our first action.

Incidentally the 'Jerries' were JU 88's, and the siren went ten minutes after it was all over.

37, Woodbantwick Rd
Lower Sydenham
S. S. 26
17. 8. 40

Dear Bill & Les,

Thanks for the letter, I enjoyed it very much. Just as I was finishing reading it on Thursday evening and wondering what I could write to you about I heard a faint "grumble" of aeroplane motors. I took no notice however and went upstairs to mums bedroom to get a clean collar.

While up there I looked out of the window in the direction of Croydon (force of habit) and beheld about a dozen machines dropping out of the haze. I thought they were British until I saw ...

d — great bombs drop from the first one. (I've just filled the pen up).

I let out a yell which brought

The original of the letter quoted opposite

The air raid Bob saw took place on Thursday 15th August, and was the first recorded attack on London. It was very significant because it marked a change of policy on the part of the Luftwaffe. From then on all major cities were targets.

The government feared that bombing would cause a complete breakdown of morale, and that the civil population would flee in terror, but when the Blitz started a few weeks later most London families reacted with a stoic anger, and a determination to carry on as usual.

Our family was a very large one, seven boys and four girls. My mother was expecting the eleventh. Joan was the eldest of the children and was twenty-one. Then came three boys, Bob, Bill and Leslie,

Mother in 1919

Joan and Bob

twins Ian and Madeline, another boy, Allen, more twins, David and Peter, and finally Anita and Carole. The births span twenty-two years. Bob was born on 13 January 1921 in Bedwardine Road in Upper Norwood in South London, in a house shared by my parents with my father's sister Dora and her family.

My mother was christened Caroline Maud, but was always known by her second name. She was one of eight children brought up in great poverty near the Lambeth Walk in Kennington. When she was about twelve, she once told me, her mother used to send her to the West End to collect the family bread for the week. She had to fill up a pillow

Father, James Hodgson – an accredited War Correspondent with The March of Time (1942)

case with stale bread given out by kindly restaurateurs. She was a negative cutter working at Pathé Frères in Soho when she met my father, James Hodgson. He too had survived a difficult childhood, as the youngest of a family of three children whose father had parted from his mother when he was very small. They were also very poor, and he told of being left at home as a child, without food, when his mother, a nurse, went on duty early in the morning. He used to go out into the fields near Edmonton and forage for carrots as he went to school. In 1905, at the age of fourteen, he had joined one of the pioneer British film companies, Warwick Trading, and had learned many of the skills of this new industry before specialising as a cameraman. An energetic and enterprising young man, he joined the Royal Flying Corps early in 1915 and took part in the development of aerial photography at Farnborough before being posted to the Middle East, where he spent the rest of the War as a photographic officer and observer with bomber squadrons in Mesopotamia and Palestine. After the War he returned to film-making as a cameraman, and eventually became Editor of a newsreel, *British Screen News*. In 1935 he joined *The March of Time* and subsequently directed many of their films including the wartime *Britain's RAF*.

At the beginning of September 1940 my parents had become increasingly worried about the danger to all of us if we remained in London. The south east of London was directly in the flight path of German bombers as they flew in to attack the docks and the city. Biggin Hill, a major fighter base, was less than ten miles from where we lived and we saw some of the fierce aerial combats of the Battle of Britain in the skies over our heads.

In early September, my brother Bill went to a second school camp on a farm near Eynsford in Kent. He went with one of the teachers, Harry Rée, and his wife, to help set it up. Harry Rée taught French at Beckenham Grammar School: later in the war he was parachuted into France where he fought with the French resistance.

On Saturday, 7 September, Bill returned home. In the middle of the afternoon he was lying in the bath when he heard the noise of aero engines. There had been a raid the previous day so my father put his head round the bathroom door and told Bill to get out of the bath quickly. 'They're on their way again,' he said.

Bill went to the window to see what was happening. The German bombers in their wide 'V' formations reminded him of flights of swans. My father took his ciné camera, and, with Bob, drove off to film the raid. Leslie, who was fifteen, put on his ARP tin helmet and rushed out to his fire-watching post. Since we had no shelter in the house my mother gathered the smaller children around her, and we all crouched by the stairs.

The next twenty-four hours were the worst London had yet known. Wave after wave of Heinkel and Dornier bombers headed towards the docks, where they dropped massive amounts of high-explosive and incendiary bombs.

After a lull in the late afternoon they returned to continue their

James Hodgson, on location shooting 'Britain's RAF'. In the background a Whitley bomber.

destruction for most of the night. Bill had gone to see a girl friend. As he cycled back heard the whine of a falling bomb. He jumped off his bicycle and lay by a church wall for cover. The bomb fell some distance away, making a terrifying chest-shaking thump as it exploded. Leslie heard another bomb fall a few hundred yards away from his ARP Post and went to investigate. He found a young girl sitting by the body of her soldier friend, weeping. He had been killed by falling masonry.

All the family spent a terrifying night lying on the floor of the sitting room. No one slept. They listened to the sound of bombs falling, sometimes distant, sometimes close, wondering where the next would be. Over 400 people were killed that night and 1600 seriously injured.

My father drove Bill back to Eynsford the next day and left him there. For the next week Bill saw the bombers flying in towards London, and the dog-fights between their escorts and the Spitfires

Bob in his new uniform, taken
in 1941 at Loudwater in
Hertfordshire where our family
went to avoid the bombing.

and Hurricanes of Fighter Command. He was very worried about
what was happening at home, and made numerous attempts to
telephone, but could never get through. On the following Saturday
the camp ended and he cycled back home. When he arrived he was
alarmed to find the house locked up and deserted. Mr Shaw, our next
door neighbour, so disapproved of the noisy and difficult Hodgson
children that he had not spoken to any of us for many years. Now he
came out into his front garden and reluctantly broke his silence. He
told Bill that we had all moved away and that my father was waiting
for him at his sister Dora's house in Upper Norwood. My father drove
Bill to Hertfordshire.

He had found a house at Loudwater, near Chorley Wood, and

taken us out of the main area of danger. Bob went on with his job in the dark rooms of Kay's Film Laboratories. He did not like it very much, and spent all his spare time pursuing his interest in flying. His main hobby was making model aircraft from balsa wood and tissue paper. He even designed his own. At the end of September, he went to the RAF Recruiting Office in Kingsway and volunteered for aircrew. He was just one of the thousands of young men attracted by the glamour and excitement of this new method of warfare. Flying demanded brains and ability, and only men of the highest calibre were selected. The losses suffered by the RAF in 1940 and the need for a huge increase in numbers required for any major offensive against Germany meant that men from widely differing social backgrounds were thrown together to become the new elite of the RAF.

In January 1941, Bob at last received his call up papers. He left his job and took a special train from Kings Cross to Bedford. There, he and his fellow recruits were taken on to the RAF Reception Centre at Cardington.

30.1.41.

Dear Mum,

I have put no address at the top because you cannot write to me here as I shall be posted somewhere else pretty soon. I arrived here at 6 p.m. and after waiting for about half an hour, was taken to a building and given a bolster, knife and fork etc. along with some other blokes and am quite happy about it. Well don't worry about me, everything is alright.

Keep smiling,
Your loving son Bob

The 'blokes' he referred to were to become his closest friends for most of his training.

My two particular cronies are named Alf Kitchen and Hugh somethingorother. We call Alf Tubby. He is not fat but very well built. Hugh is nearly as long as me but he is fair.

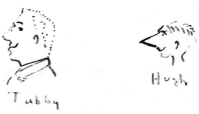

Bob often drew little sketches like these in his letters, mainly for the amusement of the younger members of the family.

The recruits were sent on to Bridgnorth in Shropshire within a week. In a reference to the author, who was then four years old, he wrote:

> If David still snores tell him that its no good joining the RAF for he would have thirty pairs of boots thrown at him the first night here.

He continued:

> We left Cardington last Wednesday at about 9.30 and after a six hour journey we arrived at Bridgnorth station. Here we got rid of our kitbags and then . . . we had to march about three miles to the camp. We made this march, mostly uphill, through snow and slush and in a blinding snowstorm. I tell yer, by the time we arrived we were properly 'browned off'.
>
> On top of this we had to wait about an hour to collect our kitbags again and since we had had no meal since 6.30 that morning, well . . . one man even called an NCO a B———y pig! I believe they realised how we felt though, for they let this go by.
>
> Now we have been here for a day though, we have decided that its much better than Cardington. The meals are bigger and better, the beds are warmer and we have hot and cold water in the wash house as well as baths and showers. To counteract this however, the discipline is much stricter although our Flight Sergeant is a very nice chap and does not bark at one yet.
>
> Today we had three lectures, one on gas, another on the rifle, and the last on PT. This last one was given by a Corporal who is really a decent chap. He told us not to mind being called all the blank blank blanks under the sun as the instructors did not really mean it. Some of us are going for a cross-country run next Wednesday with him and he told us that if he has a hard morning, all he does is run for a quarter of a hour and then finds a convenient wall to sit and smoke on!
>
> We did a bit of marching this morning and it was rather amusing. On every movement we have to shout 'one', or 'one pause two'. Unfortunately there is a chap from South America — Brazil — who does not understand the orders very well. When we were given the order, 'Salute to the left flank,' he saluted with his left hand!'

He ended the letter with this drawing and comment.

P.S. Please try and get me some R.A.F. socks as the service ones are miles to small for me and most uncomfortable. b...y great boots; uncomfortable; my heel; heel of sock

Bob was six feet four inches tall, and took size twelve boots.

The training that followed in the next few weeks was the usual combination of drill, rifle instruction, discipline and fitness. With Bob this seems to have produced sore feet and great hunger.

> By the way a chap in the next bunk has had about six parcels of grub since he's been here. I don't want to cadge at this time, but if you could possibly tickle the folks up I sure would appreciate it. Honestly the Naffy is getting lousy now. You are only allowed two cakes a night, one at dinner time, and there is no chocolate at all now. There has been none for the last two weeks. It's funny, but sweets are a great comfort to one on service.
>
> Bob, Feast, and I went to Bridgnorth last Saturday and after we had scoured the town for chocolate, which was unobtainable, we went into the Bridge Cafe. Here we ordered ham, eggs, chips, bread and butter, and a pot of tea. Well, after waiting for an hour and a half we were served. The tea was in silver teapots and the bread was thin, the ham was delicious and we really enjoyed ourselves. Not the least part of our enjoyment was sitting at a table with a cloth instead of hard wooden benches.
>
> Last Sunday I went to my first Church Parade and I was number one man being the tallest. By the way we are allowed an extra hour in bed on Sundays, rising at 7.30 instead of 6.30.
>
> It's now nearly tea time, which is at 4.30, so I'll finish this later on.
>
> I'm just back from tea. Tonight, wonder of wonders, I obtained two teas by joining in the queue twice. Simple eh, but you have to watch out for the mess orderly.

Towards the end of his preliminary training at Bridgnorth, Bob injured the achilles tendon of his right heel, and was confined to his barracks.

> I feel very disconsolate at the moment. The other chaps are discussing what they are going to do in town this afternoon and I can't do B.A. except hang around the 'Naffy' (canteen).

Tubby fell on his nose when he was five years old, and spread it all over his face. Derek is always ill. He has two days in bed, followed by two days light duty, followed by two days light duty. He is our extreme 'right wingist.'

Bob[2] as you already know is an English-born Canadian. We are always chipping him about his accent. He says 'champeens' for champions, 'turble' for terrible, and many other mispronunciations. His favourite reply is, 'What's good enough for Canadian High School is good enurf ferr me.' His great ambition is to be a Spitfire pilot.

Hugh is another tall, fair and not very handsome chap like myself. He is also a great cricketer, according to his account. He wants to be a bomber pilot.

There are two other chaps in the hut with harmonicas and we make quite a row between us of an evening. I don't know whether to press my trousers, or go to sleep, or have a bath. Since another chap is using the iron, and my right foot is done up in sticking plaster, I think I'll go to sleep.

In February 1941, as Bob was pounding the parade ground of Bridgnorth, my mother had her eleventh child, Carole. The news obviously made Bob think about the family.

> 51 Hut, 4 Wing,
> RAF Station Bridgnorth,
> Salop.
> Saturday 8th March, 1941

Dear Joan,

How are mum and the baby doing? Is Nini still thrilled with her or is she getting jealous now? Has Ian finished his Lysander yet? Old 'Tubby' has double jointed arms and when he stretches them out they look just like a Lysander's wings.

Have Madeline and Alan got over their injections yet? How is Mad's knitting getting on? Does she still believe in pre-shrinking the wool by salt water before use?

As for Dave and Pete, so long as they still 'bomb battleships,' I know that they are OK.

Tell Bill to hurry up and write again. Providing he can go sick half the time, tell him, the RAF's not too bad. All the blokes here are extreme leftists, and to listen to them makes me wonder how the devil we are going to win this war.

The family at Loudwater

By early 1941 the RAF had had to absorb a tremendous battering from the German fighters and ground defences. It is poignant to compare the cheerful hope expressed in these letters with the reality of what was happening. The men of Fighter Command had fought a courageous defensive campaign to win the Battle of Britain, but the men of Bomber command — no less courageous — had not been able to carry out the offensive role with anything approaching the effect that had been claimed would be possible. In 1928, Lord Trenchard had written a memorandum to his fellow Chiefs of Staff in which he put forward his theory of the Strategic Air Offensive. He argued that in modern warfare it is necessary to defeat an enemy nation, not just its armed forces. To do this we would have to attack the centres of production, transportation and communication, and that long-range bombers would be able to carry this out. At the time it was believed that such raids would also lead to a rapid collapse in the morale of the civilian population; law and order would break down and the enemy would be forced to sue for peace. It was a doctrine that was much criticised by the other services. The way air power should be used had been much debated since the end of the First World War, and many people thought that bombing civilian targets was quite immoral. The Army and the Navy both believed that aeroplanes should be used to support troop movements, and protect fleets and convoys. The RAF wanted an independent role. This debate was of great significance because it directly led to the development of the types of aircraft that were to be used ten years later.

In the early 'thirties the Air Ministry laid down the specifications for the long-range bombers that went into action against German military targets in 1939. They were to be capable of precision bombing and also be self-protecting. As such they would require no long-range fighter escort so none was developed. It was considered that with their turrets of .303 inch machine guns they would be more than capable of dealing with enemy fighters, and they would be able to fly above anti-aircraft gunfire. Nothing could stop them getting through, and in daylight they would be able to find their targets and knock out factories, oil installations, and similar industrial areas with ease. However, when war eventually came, we had lagged so far behind the Germans in aircraft production that such an offensive operation was for the time being out of the question. In September 1939 the RAF had at its disposal 608 fighters, against 1,215 of the Luftwaffe, and 536 bombers against 2,130.

Trenchard's theories were enthusiastically followed by his successors, and the war against Germany was the first real opportunity to put them into practice. A second generation of bombers, vastly superior to the Hampdens, Whitleys, and Wellington 1s was rapidly being developed. Meanwhile raids were attempted on naval targets at Wilhelmshaven in December 1939, and the advancing German armies in Belgium in May 1940. Tragically for the aircrews these attacks were disastrous. The low level approaches that were necessary against the bridgeheads at Maastricht and Sedan were hopeless in the face of very accurate groundfire, and cost the lives of over half the men sent, to little effect. High-level bombing was tried at Wilhelmshaven, but the Germans picked up the approaching bombers on their radar (which the Air Ministry denied existed) and directed their fighters to where they were operating. The fighters were armed with 30 mm cannons, which had far greater power and range, than the .303 inch machine guns used by the bombers. It was a brilliantly clear day, and with such good visibility the fighters had a relatively easy task to find and destroy the slow-moving Wellingtons. Only ten out of twenty four managed to get back.

Furthermore, it had proved to be almost impossible to bomb accurately under combat conditions. No damage had been inflicted on the German warships.

Following a number of other unsuccessful raids, it became clear that the losses from daylight attacks would be catastrophic. For a long time the Air Chiefs had had in mind the possibility of bombing the Ruhr. But it became obvious that our planes simply would not get there in daylight. So from the middle of 1940 it was decided to concentrate our efforts at night. For the aircrews however, night bombing presented great difficulties. Effective radio and radar navigation aids had yet to be developed, and they had to try to find their targets mainly with estimates of their position by dead reckoning based on course settings and wind speeds. Even if they got there, it was nearly impossible to know exactly where bombs were falling over a blacked-out city.

By January 1941, when Bob and his fellow airmen joined the RAF there were real question marks about its ability to inflict significant damage on the Germans. It was the only means of striking directly at Hitler, and both for international political reasons, and for our own morale, it was necessary to show we were doing something. But the cost was to be enormous both in terms of our financial and industrial resources, and in men's lives.

Chapter Two
Initial Training Wing

On 14 March Bob was posted to RAF Swanton Morley, near Dereham in Norfolk. He had been selected for aircrew training, but there was a delay before the start of the course. In his first letter home, he wrote:

> I received 34/- this morning after saluting very smartly. The method of pay here seems to be more generous. I am still owed two pounds eleven shillings though. I expect that this will be made up when I get seven days leave. We have not been doing much except clean out the ablutions. Yesterday we, that is Bob[2], Hugh and myself, went for a stroll round the aerodrome. It was quite a walk I can tell you. We had a good look at the kites which all had pet names such as Popeye, Jane, Pinocchio, and Old Faithful. They also have amusing drawings on them.
>
> Last Wednesday we saw the educational officer and arranged to study maths. I have got the hang of Logs and Trigonometry already owing to the help of Bob[2] Wells. As I said before, I'm not going to fail my pilot's course through any inability to do a few sums after going through three or four months of this sort of thing.

After his first week's leave, he returned to Swanton Morley, where the occasional aircraft recognition course was interspersed with long hours in an airfield defence gunpit.

> Life here is still pretty boring. I think this is about the windiest aerodrome on earth. It is so cutting that I wear the Balaclava helmet and about six scarves as well as a leather jacket. the wind still gets through that lot.
>
> We have some fun in the gunpit shooting at partridges with which this country abounds. Uncle Sam, a bloke who hails from Boston, Mass., hit one the other day and took it to the cook house to be cooked. Needless to say it wasn't. Every post, tincan, or tree trunk around us is riddled. We even set one alight the other day with incendiary bullets. We use the rifles with which we were issued and any ammo which we can knock off. This accounts for the variety which we use — ball, armour-piercing, tracer, incendiary, and soft-nosed. Don't spread this around though.
>
> The kites round here spend so much time on the ground that its a wonder they don't grow roots. The Squadron has, according to Uncle

Sam, just invested in some new shovels in order to dig them out for the next offensive.

Well, I'll wind up as usual with a sketch for the kids.

On Wednesday 16 and Saturday 19 April 1941, the heaviest raids yet fell on South London. The attack on the 16th was particularly savage. The sirens went at about nine o'clock in the evening, and the first bombs started to fall in the Kentish villages just outside Bromley. As the raid progressed, huge amounts of high explosive, incendiary bombs and landmines rained down on Bromley, Beckenham, Sydenham, Lewisham and Deptford. Three days later the raid was repeated on Greenwich, Woolwich and the docks. The attack had been carried out by 700 bombers. On the Wednesday alone, 900 tons of high explosive and 150,000 incendiaries were dropped on these largely residential areas. We were still safely out of the way in Hertfordshire, but when Bob read about it he was very angry.

> How did the blitz affect you the other night? It made me bloody wild when I read about it. I won't bring any bombs back if I ever get over there. London's night of judgment eh! I'll get there if I break my neck learning to fly.

On the 14 May Bob's preliminary ground training as a pilot began. He was posted to 20 Operational Training Unit based at Lossiemouth, near Aberdeen:

> We arrived at Lossie at twelve o'clock. Twenty-three hours on a train — we were glad to get out. It was sunshining at the time, and the little village of grey stone houses looked very cheerful. A bus came down and off we went to the camp. Here we got out first shock. Wooden huts! Wooden huts after our solid, warm draughtless blocks at Swanton. Was there ever a man dismayed. Not half there wasn't.

Bob's sketch of the result of a boxing match. Sport filled in much of the time inevitably spent waiting.

Well, in the usual RAF fashion, we were kept hanging about. Eventually a corporal was put in charge of us and we had some lunch. This [lunch] wasn't up to much either. We shoved into the Naffy and got our second shock. It was dirty, there were about ten cups between a hundred, and all the girls, all of them, were ugly and had accents you could cut with a knife.

The corporal in charge of us is an Irishman by the name of Lea. He is a liar (he told us he had been in the RAF for nine years and he's only twenty one), he borrows money from all of us and forgets to pay it back, and doesn't know the first thing about foot drill (gives all the orders on the wrong foot). In short he's a twirp who fancies his luck.

It appears we are here on a pre-ITW course. This is an entirely new scheme, and we have the distinction of being the first batch of aircrew to go through. We will be given a course equivalent to that in an Initial Training Wing, and according to what courses we have passed here, so they will be knocked off the ITW course. Of course, if you fail an exam here you will not be kicked out. You just carry on until you pass. We have to do PT and square bashing as well (worse luck).

Bob's training at Lossiemouth largely consisted of classes in mathematics, morse or signals, and armaments. At the weekends he and his friends would wander round the local town:

Bob Wells and I went to Elgin yesterday. We left camp at two, but had to wait half an hour for a bus. We went to the Church Canteen (sandwiches at 1d each) and filled up. After this we wandered round a bit, went and had a drink, and went to the cinema.

Lossiemouth, as I said, is a small fishing village with a population of about two thousand. It is typically Scottish, grey stone houses, clean and tidy and rather cold looking. It has a nice cinema with a cafe attached. The fishing fleet is quite large, and we witnessed a fish sale when we were there. You know, '4 pounds blah blah blah!!' They were the only words which we could understand.

The sky is always full of planes. Hurricanes continually burn the air up. I saw a Martlet yesterday. It was going like a bat out of hell, full out I should think. There are also a couple of Curtiss P35s and Tomahawks here. The Curtisses are very small — the Tomahawk being about the same size as a Hurricane.

Towards the end of June he was moved to a small camp with what must have been the most unlikely name in the whole of the RAF:

> RAF Station,
> Oakwood Tea Gardens,
> Elgin,
> Moray,
> Scotland.
> Wednesday afternoon.

Dear Joan,

As you will see our address has changed drastically. We have moved clean out of camp to this spot two miles the other side of Elgin. It is like heaven: the Oakwood Tea Gardens consist of a large, and about a dozen small, chalets. They are built of wood and covered with small logs in the form of rustic work and varnished light brown. The roofs are tiled in red and altogether the place looks like one of Walt Disney's 'Seven Dwarfs' houses. It is set back from the road amid the trees which have just bloomed, and is altogether a really smashing place to be.

The weather is beautiful with a capital B. I am sitting outside on the veranda with only a singlet and trousers on. The sun is absolutely blazing down.

The bugger of it is that the chances are that we shall be moved from here within a fortnight. (Excuse my French.)

He was correct, for at the end of June they were sent to No. 9 Initial Training Wing at Stratford-on-Avon. Their accommodation was the Avonside Hotel. Bob sent a vital message to his mother:

Urgent! send my other pair of underpants whatever their condition. These RAF issues are killing in this weather. How do you like the heatwave? It comes a bit hard when you have to march at 140 to the minute in this weather. It's killing.

After what seems to have been some confusion as to exactly what was going to be done with the cadets, the course began in earnest:

It's started. Up at 6.15, parade for breakfast at 6.55, a mile to march for it, and twenty minutes to wait when you get there, a mile back again and its eight o'clock, time for another parade, no time to do anything personal (faeces etc.), away we march again, right across Stratford to the RAF occupied school for maths. 2 hrs of maths, all back as fast as possible, then back to the Memorial Theatre for an address by the CO; back in the hotel, hour of aircraft recognition on the lawn and it's 12.40, time for lunch. Away we march, another wait for lunch, on parade at 1.40, for the MO lecture, and so on, parade after parade until 6. Tea at 6.15 and an hour of private study after that. Have to be in by 10 so it's not worth going out. Go for a swim in the river, and then polish buttons and boots and shave for morning. Wash my socks and boy! are my dogs tired. 8 weeks of this nearly. Is it worth it?

It's now Thursday morning. I received the parcel containing my pants yesterday, and they are OK — in fact they're swell.

Friday. Boy! what a morning. Our NCO in/c is a proper sod! He has no sense of humour and on the slightest provocation he binds (moans or grumbles) like hell. He stopped us on the way to dinner and let the other flights go in front of us because some one whispered in the ranks. All the boys are well and truly browned off. Owing to the weather my feet are giving me hell, right foot especially.

Sunday. Went sick yesterday with a couple of blisters to my eternal shame. I thought I was through with that sort of thing. Still I've missed Church Parade through it.

Over the next few weeks, Bob's letters mainly contained requests for cigarettes and the odd item of clothing. He still hadn't received his laundry from Swanton Morley! He managed to pass his maths, navigation, and other essential examinations, and on 16 August was posted to No. 16 EFTS (Elementary Flying Training School) at RAF Burnaston, near Derby.

As Bob and his fellow airmen started their flying instruction, a report by Mr D. Butt, a member of Lord Cherwell's secretariat, was handed to the Prime Minister. Cherwell was Churchill's personal scientific adviser, and had asked Butt to examine the accuracy of Bomber Command's reports of the damage they claimed to be inflicting on the Germans. Butt looked at the intelligence photographs taken on a hundred separate raids on twenty-eight targets during the months of June and July. He found that in attacks against the Ruhr, only one plane in ten managed to get within five miles of the aiming point, and of those that did, none was able to drop their bombs with any real likelihood of them falling within a thousand yards of the target. On cloudy nights the proportion dropped to one in fifteen. This came as a shock to Churchill and the War Cabinet, who had largely accepted the Air Chiefs' estimates of the destructive power of Bomber Commands sorties, and their probable effect on German morale.

It was quite obvious from the report that the vast resources being put into Bomber Command were not being effectively used. The German Blitz on British cities had removed the moral scruples many people felt about bombing civilian targets. But it did raise the awkward point that the Blitz, far from causing a collapse of civilian morale, had provoked an angry desire to hit back. Why should the Germans react differently?

The main conclusion to be drawn from the Butt report, however, was that precision bombing at night was not possible. New urgency had to be put into the efforts to produce navigation aids and bombing techniques that would enable our bombers to have some real effect. The destruction of whole areas round industrial targets was the only workable policy. And as the Germans improved their air defences as the war went on, the task became increasingly formidable. An acceptable loss rate had been calculated on the chances of a crew surviving their minimum tour of thirty operations. If the loss rate was 7½% per operation, an aircrew had only a one-in-ten chance of surviving: 5% was considered to be the maximum rate that a squadron could stand without serious damage to its morale. Most of the young airmen under training with Bob would not see the end of their tour.

One of the main reasons for the continuation of raids on Germany was that at this point in the war, it was the only way we could strike back directly. This policy was sustained by the belief still held by the Air Chiefs, even after the Butt report, that they alone could win the War. New plans were drawn up and presented to Churchill in September 1941. The Directorate of Bomber Operations at the Air Ministry calculated that if continuous attacks were mounted on the 43 German towns with populations of more than 100,000, their industry would collapse within six months. To carry out this attack would require 4,000 bombers. In a sharp reply, Churchill said:

It is very disputable whether bombing by itself will be a decisive factor in the present War. On the contrary, all we have learnt since the War began shows that its effects are greatly exaggerated. There is no doubt the British people have been stimulated and strengthened by the attack made upon them so far. Secondly, it seems very likely that the ground defences and night fighters will overtake the air attack. Thirdly, calculating the number of bombers necessary to achieve a hypothetical and indefinite tasks, it should be noted that only a quarter of our bombs hit the targets. Consequently an increase in accuracy of bombing to 100% would in fact raise our bombing force to four times its strength. The most we can hope is that it will be a heavy and I trust a seriously increasing annoyance.

Chapter Three
Learning to Fly

16 EFTS
RAF Burnaston

Dear Bill,

Perhaps it would be as well to give a short description of this place before I go on. Before the war it was a civilian Flying Training School. It is still run by civilians, but the flying instructors are all in the RAF. Navigation classes are all taken by civilian instructors. My instructor is F/O Samson. He is a DFC, what for I don't know and I don't intend to ask.

I started flying on Monday. I went up first for 20 mins. to gain experience. After about an hour I went up again and was allowed to handle the controls. At first it wasn't so easy but after a time with the instructors voice cooing in my ear, 'Stick to the left, left rudder, stick forward,' etc., I began to pick it up. After about thirty minutes we landed.

Next day (Tuesday) I tried turning, and managed pretty well. Incidentally you do centralise the stick after banking, and even give it opposite aileron. You hardly touch the rudder at all. To come out of a turn, opposite aileron and when straight, rudder. After a time you do both together. As for straight flying, that comes automatically, much the same as you joggle the wheel of a car. After we had landed, Samson said that when he saw me, six feet four etc. he thought I'd be as ham handed as anything, but I seemed quite OK. I told him I'd made models and we had quite a chat.

Today, after we had unstuck, he straight away gave me the controls, and told me to keep her climbing. After making a circuit of the 'drome, he showed me how to land, throttle back, flaps down, tail trim back, etc. After we came down he showed me how to take off, and up we went again, another circuit and 'You've got her, take her in'. It shook me but I had a crack at it and managed it a treat with him helping me. Then I had to take her off, open her up, left rudder to stop her swinging, ease the stick back at about 60, nose down a bit to pick up speed and then climb at 70. I had one more crack at taking off and four more landings, all with a little assistance from him.

I also know what a stall feels like. We did three, one with the engine off, one with the engine at normal, and lastly with her wide open. It's a peculiar sensation — you leave your inside way up behind you, while down below are a few cows grazing peacefully. The nose gradually goes up until it towers above you, and then, whoosh, down it goes, one wing drops, kick back the rudder, centralise the stick and ease her back opening the throttle. Well, that's flying to a beginner and it seems to be fairly easy.

The weather here is pretty lousy, especially today. We are near the Pennines, the watershed of England. You can see the rain coming a mile off. The clouds hang right down to the ground. We have to fly between showers.

Our billets are pretty lousy, being in a musty old building in Repton School of 'Mr Chips' fame. Stan Holloway and I went into Derby on Sunday and again on Tuesday. It's not a bad town being quite big, and there are 15 Cinemas and much pretty women. We have strict instructions to keep off too much beer (or wine, women, and song as the C/O puts it.)

The plane Bob was learning to fly was a Miles Magister, a low-winged monoplane in which the pupil sat behind the pilot, with open cockpits.

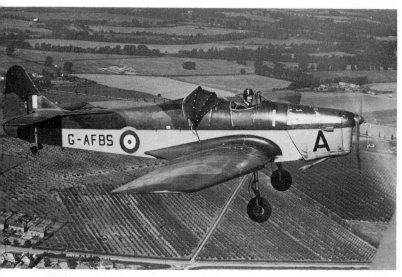

Miles Magister (*Imperial War Museum*)

I still can't make consistently good landings but I've plenty of time yet. Since I last wrote I've done 8 hrs 40 mins. One hour of this consisted of cross-country flying which I quite enjoyed. Flying by compass is pretty easy. You set the course on the grid ring which holds two parallel wires about an inch apart across the middle, and swing the kite until the compass needle, which is enclosed in an alcohol-filled container below it, is parallel with the grid wires, the north end of the compass against the north end of the grid ring. You then keep the aircraft straight by looking at the horizon, with an occasional glance at the compass. You treat the needle as your rudder bar and if the port end of the needle swings towards you, you press the left rudder and vice versa. This is not an official secret by the way.

Landing, as I said before is the worst, or rather the hardest part. I get the approaches OK, but the final touch down isn't so easy. I always know beforehand whether the landing is going to be OK or not. It's just a matter of practice, and I am getting better at it every time I go up. Every time I come flicking in across the road I think of the old days when we used to stand outside Croydon airport and watch the oil-flecked bellies of the 5/- trippers slide across the sky fifteen feet above us. It's funny how you notice details from the air, the car with two headlamps masks going by underneath, the kid in the red coat, or a wreck of an old Morris Cowley on its side where somebody left it after landing on top of it. You feel you are flying when you are only a couple of hundred feet up.

Stan H and I went to Nottingham on Saturday, after being out till 2 o'clock in the morning. We went to a dance in Derby on Friday, and I messed up my pedal extremities trying to dance in rubber-soled boots. Stan was in a little better shape, and after we had seen a girl home to Normanton, three miles outside Derby, we were both in a bad way. We've somewhat recovered since, but I'll not try that lark any more.

Touching on the subject of women as you put it, once does get a certain amount of relief in seeing and talking to some one with a different face, no uniform, and who doesn't talk about kites, spins, etc. etc. The only one I've seen worth putting oneself out for works in, or rather serves behind a milkbar (yes, milk)!

Many of the letters that were sent to Bob by members of my family have been lost in the intervening years. The earliest letter that now exists from a member of the family to Bob is dated September 1941. It was from Bill, and clearly reflects the anxiety felt by my mother.

I was glad to get your letter to me. Your last one to Mum came this evening and she was very happy and relieved to hear the news. I guess she saw you all the time as a sort of condemned man already, (and she was probably right). Is it definite you will be an instructor, and does it carry a comission? Do you still want to 'drop shit' on Germany as you so aptly put it? Plenty of silly buggers can do that, but they couldn't teach their grandmothers to suck eggs. I should imagine that an instructor's life is very pleasant, but ultimately rather monotonous. Some trembling plonks (or is it sproggs?) all making the same trembling bloomers etc. But as a bomber pilot, or a fighter pilot you'd only be one in 50,000 (we hope).

Bill was echoing wishful thinking on the part of my parents, who

would have been aware of the growing losses being suffered by Bomber Command.

On the 1 November 1941 Bob was posted to RAF Shawbury, in Shropshire. He started to fly Airspeed Oxfords — twin-engined training aircraft.

Up here the weather let up last Monday, and we flew in all sorts of shit imaginable on Wednesday. Net result four and a half hours dual for yours truly. I don't like these Oxfords a lot. You don't seem to be connected directly with the controls as in a light aeroplane. They bump like hell on take-off, and land like a ton of bricks. In level flight they fly themselves if you trim them properly. We have been using an airfield which you could hardly land a Maggie in. If you go solo off of this you are pretty good. That's what my instructor says. He is only a young bloke, likes Yank cars and his old man has a Packard. He doesn't bind a bit and lets you get on with the job, unless you're heading for a (closed) hangar. He says I could have gone solo but for the weather. I suppose it would make a difference if you could see more than fifty yards ahead.

We, 41 Course, have got in the Chief Ground Instructor's hair. Apparently we are the most undisciplined course yet. That's what they

Airspeed Oxford (*IWM*)

said at Burnaston. At any rate just to show there's no ill feeling, he has inserted one drill period a day in our lecture programme. This has never been done before, so we are pioneers in body if not in spirit. We do one day's flying and one day's lectures alternately.

Christmas 1941 at RAF Shawbury was a fairly muted affair.

Christmas at Shawbury wasn't much cop. Apart from one or two evenings when we went pub crawling it was pretty tame. We were given Christmas Day off so we all stayed in bed until half past eleven and crawled out to lunch. We had dinner with turkey, Xmas pud etc, and tanked it up in the Sergeants Mess. Even Tubby, a confirmed TT got half canned (out of sheer brassed-offness).

On New Year's Eve, Jimmy Taaffe and I drank a pub dry of Scotch (or Irish) and then I gate-crashed the Caledonian Dance (the most exclusive of all Scottish Clubs) with a guy named Jock Hamilton. He pinched the ticket which I used, and he got in by virtue of his Scotch accent. We got back to camp at two o'clock in the morning on the back of a flood-light trailer from our night flying airfield.

I am now broke, but who cares, I shall be on a charge in a few days as I was knocked off by Red Caps [Military Police] in Shrewsbury on Saturday night. I had my coat undone and my respirator on my shoulder and my hands in my pockets. Jimmy Taaffe was doing the same but while they were putting the heat on me, he re-adjusted himself. I shall get 7 days, I expect.

Sgts. Mess
Shawbury
Jan. 1942

Dear Joan,

The past week has been most uneventful. Oh yes with my usual efficient manner of getting whatever is going I grabbed a cold in the old tum tum and believe me I thought I'd got the usual 21st birthday complaint, appendicitis. I hope to be mended by next week end. It seems a hell of a long time since I was last home.

As for the charges I was on, I scraped out of them. The CGI who at the best of times is a silly old ass made a complete balls up of the charge sheet and put down another bloke's charge and punishment against my name. As the punishment was only a ticking-off (admonishment) rather than lose face by altering the sheet he dismissed me with a caution. While I was up with him, I missed a Link trainer period and the officer i/c was all for giving me 6 days for it. By dint of much talking I managed to get out of this. On getting back to the billet I found that the SP's were after me for not putting up the blackouts. Some silly ass had shoved a bulb in and switched on without looking out of the windows. However they got their teeth into another bloke for that, and once more I breathed freely. Houdini's got nothing on me as an escapologist (touch wood).

While most of Bob's letters are concerned with his own experience on camp, and what was going on in the family, he occasionally wrote (mostly to Bill) about what was going on in the war in Europe and the Far East. In a letter to Bill at the end of January 1942 he speculated about the way the war was proceeding:

The Russians seem to be shoving the Nazis back. I am now waiting for the retaking of Kharkov. It will be the first big town the Russians have captured. The Germans however seem to be holding a road and railway junction SE of Moscow, but I think will be encircled in time. Their defensive line is not very straight. In fact they seem to be retiring in disorder — not at all strategically. It looks as though Malaya will be a repetition of that. No air support or anti-tank guns and armoured forces. Just no foresight on the part of the persons responsible. Singapore will get it in the neck shortly.

In that estimation Bob was absolutely correct. On 8 February, the Japanese forces that had overrun Malaya in the previous two months launched their invasion of the island. A week later, the British Commander-in-Chief General Percival surrendered as the enemy

Bob.   Alf Kitchin.   Hugh Feast.

troops reached the suburbs of the city of Singapore. Food was running short, and the water supply was about to be cut off.

As for Kharkov, it was another year before the city was recaptured by the Russians. Although the German offensive had been halted by the Russian winter and a fierce counterattack, it was resumed in June. By September, the German Panzer divisions had advanced on a wide front, and were within fifteen miles of Stalingrad. The failure to take that city marked the turning point of the war. On 19 November the Russians launched their counter-offensive, and as the Germans were slowly driven back, their defeat became inevitable, not only in Russia, but in the rest of Europe also.

In the early part of 1942, however, the defeat of Hitler must have seemed a long way off. Perhaps because they were still cushioned from the reality of what was going on in Europe, and with the prospect of going into action themselves as yet distant, the trainee aircrews were cheerfully pre-occupied with the immediate problems of learning to fly, and coping with women. It is easy to forget how young most of them were. Bob had had his twenty-first birthday in January, and like many of this fellow airmen, was rather shy and inexperienced with the opposite sex. The proximity of large numbers of WAAFs no doubt helped the situation; the odd romance seems to have blossomed, in spite of the 'friendly interest' being shown by colleagues:

> Hughie Feast is going out with a WAAF from the Station Sick Quarters — a dental orderly. I believe he is taking her seriously as, whereas when we chipped him at first he took it with equanimity, he now looses his wool and consequently gets chipped even more. We are trying to arrange that I meet her in Shrewsbury and look at the furniture shop in full view of Hughie. Tubby has written to Drages, Truefords, Barringtons and even Smarts in Feast's name asking for catalogues. He even asked Barringtons to send a catalogue of engagement rings to Hughie's home address to give his parents a shock. Just innocent fun.

In a letter to Joan a few weeks later he wrote:

> Flying has started again with a rush. Yesterday Jimmy Taaffe and myself went on a cross-country which took up the best part of three hours. We got down as far as Oxford. I was the navigator and Jimmy was the pilot. I gave him courses to steer and he didn't do so badly — never more than 30° out at a time. At any rate we made it even if we did fly to the Bristol Channel before we realised we were following the Severn in the wrong direction. Today the weather has shut down again, mist, rain, so once more no flying.
>
> I was glad to hear that you are busy in the house. It must make a change from sitting in an armchair, or on the boss's knee in the office and doing precisely B.A.
>
> The glamour boys are still cracking along. This morning we had our seventh lecture telling us that 41 course (glamour boys) were not taking sufficient pride in their bearing.
>
> Poor old Hughie, he walked into the station bug hutch (cinema) the other night, and as luck was not in his way, I happened to see him. (He had his WAAF with him.) I yelled out 'Hughie' in a falsetto voice, and about twenty other members of our course, Tubby, Jimmy, etc., all started booing and hissing. Boy! was his face red. Every time there was a love scene in the flick Tubby screamed out 'Bags of dual, Feast!' Last night Hughie was to meet his WAAF at 6.45. He went into the bathroom clad in his trousers only, and Tubby locked the door of his room so that he couldn't get the rest of his clothes. This episode has not closed yet.

At the end of March 1942, with the German bombing of London easing off, we moved back to the family house in Sydenham:

> Dear Mum,
>
> I suppose you are more or less settled down by now in the old house. How do you like it back there? We have managed to do another cross-country flight with myself as pilot this time and Jimmy Taaffe as

Jimmy Taaffe

navigator. We had a bit of fun on this one. I saw a sort of country mansion on some high ground about 800 feet. It was on a plateau, and at one end of its garden was a clock tower about 50 feet high, so just by way of a diversion I went down and did a steep turn round it. A little after we saw a farm where Jimmy used to stay so we beat that up, just hopping over the grain sheds and between the farm buildings. Bags of panic in the farmyard. Strictly against the regs of course. Coming back we overtook Feast and Kitching so from then on it was a sort of dog fight back to Shawbury. We beat them in on the circuit, much to Hughie's disgust.

We have also started night flying which isn't as bad as it sounds. You just can't afford to make mistakes. We use a field with runways so there isn't much room to swerve or skid when landing or taking off. It's not very comfortable over there as the 'drome is only half finished, and there is no light except for hurricane lamps.

Dear Bill,

Back at the old dump once more and feeling slightly shagged. I couldn't sleep on the train as there was an asthmatic airman in the same compartment who offended my ears most mightily with sundry whistles, snorts, and grunts. On top of this I did three hours flying this morning — instruments and formation. I was afraid to get too close in case I went to sleep on the job, and slid into him. However nothing happened and I slept most of the afternoon and was in bed till eleven this morning.

This afternoon I went up with one Ralph Miller to do bombing practice of sorts over the Camera Obscura, a clever instrument on the ground which records your bombing run. Ralph nearly piled the kite up on landing. We were cross-wind and he was drifting towards the obstructions. He shoved on full right throttle and down went the left wing decapitating sundry daisies and other wild fauna. Despite the fact that neither of us were strapped in and would probably have broken our necks if the wing had touched, we both burst out laughing once she was down on all three (after touching each one in succession about twenty times). When I landed her an hour later a Beaufighter started to taxi across the field instead of using the perimeter track, and I had to very nearly stand her on her nose to stop her in time. The attitude of the test pilots seems to be 'F . . . you Charlie, I'm alright'.

By the middle of April Bob's time at Shawbury began to draw to an end. The main skill to be perfected was night flying:

Night flying hasn't gone as well as it should. I went out to Wheaton Aston, which is where we now do our night flying on Friday night. It was a lovely night, moonlight, but the wind was a little high and slightly across the runway. I could easily have gone solo as I felt right on top of the job, but Fl.Lt. Gee wouldn't let anybody go solo because of the wind. At the risk of boring you I will try and describe a dual circuit.

We taxied up towards the taxying post with an 'erk' guiding us past dispersed aircraft, with a torch in each hand. We stop just off the flare path and quickly do our cockpit drill. I flash our identity letter and there is a blinding green flash from the duty pilot's Aldis. We can go.

Open up a little, and get into the flare path, a touch of left brake and round into the wind, uncage gyro on zero and gently open up. The flares gather speed and whip away behind us — seventy on the clock and she still sticks to the concrete. Ease back the stick and the wheels stop rumbling. As we get airborne the slight cross-wind drifts us to the right and we cross the boundary lights about fifty feet up, start initial climb at 85 and at a hundred feet retract undercart. At three hundred feet, mixture to normal, zero boost, intake to hot and switch out recognition lights. Climb to seven hundred feet with eyes glued on horizon and air speed, then begin a climbing turn onto 270°. This should bring us to a thousand feet, by the time we have reached 270° on the gyro. However we get to a thousand feet on about 290°, so throttle back and trim. Risk a quick look out to the left, and there is the flare path. Looks bloody small. Turn downwind and put the undercart down. Tap out letter on the downward rec light. Lovely, the

Aldis winks green. Mixture to rich. Flare path now behind wingtip so turn cross-wind and shove down flaps, trim for a glide of 85 and check the undercart, mixture, and loosen throttle nut.

Turn in towards flare path. Bloody fine, right in green from angle of flight indicator on flare path. Airspeed a bit high so trim back, a little rudder to take off drift. Shit! in red now, open up, green, throttle back or you'll be too high, airspeed, height, airspeed, nearly there — boundary lights slide underneath, throttle back, not too much, must keep motor on right down to deck, level off a bit, shock absorbers grunt a bit as wheels hit, shut throttles right up, wheels are biting as wind gets side of kite. Stick back, back. Suddenly the resistance goes as the tail stalls, a frantic stub of the left brake to stop the swing and it's over. The last flare comes up and we swing out of the flare path. I wonder what all the panic was for. 'Another one like that and you can go solo'. OK, but no solo for Robert as Mr Gee doesn't like the wind. Just my luck.

However by the end of May, service flying training was over. Bob received his 'wings', and moved on to the next stage of training for operations. He was posted to 24 Operational Training Unit at Honeybourne, near Evesham, in Worcestershire on 2 June.

Chapter Four
Operational Training

Honeybourne was a new purpose-built aerodrome which had been created in 1940 among the beautiful orchards and farms in the Vale of Evesham. Initially, it was used to train ferry pilots, but eventually, in March 1942, 24 OTU was set up there to train bomber pilots. It was equiped mainly with Whitleys, obsolescent twin-engined medium bombers with an effective maximum cruising speed of 165 mph, but which could carry a bomb load of 3,500 lb on sorties to the German industrial heartlands. The Ruhr still remained the prime target in the minds of the Air Chiefs, but the months that had followed the highly critical Butt report of August 1941 had been difficult for Bomber Command.

Losses mounted, and in November 1941, on two raids on Berlin, they had become unacceptably high. One in eight of the aircraft sent had failed to return. The prospect of aircrews surviving their tours of thirty operations had become extremely bleak. Activity was scaled down, and in February 1942 Sir Arthur Harris replaced Sir Richard Pierse as C-in-C Bomber Command. Harris had a very powerful and domineering personality which he used to push through his ideas about the role of the forces under his command. He saw his first task as trying to restore the credibility of the bomber squadrons, and he achieved an enormous coup in the imagination of the British public with his Thousand Bomber raid on Cologne on the 30 May 1942. He was the arch-exponent of area bombing, and eventually succeeded in building up his squadrons to the point where they were able to inflict vast damage to the fabric of most major German cities.

Together with daylight raids carried out by the USAF, they destroyed the homes of five million people, and killed an estimated three to six hundred thousand civilians. The effect on German industry was less clear, for remarkably, the production of armaments continued to increase till a few months before the ceasefire. The war historians B.H. Liddell Hart and A.J.P. Taylor, and a number of others have expressed considerable doubts as to the real value of the contribution of Bomber Command towards winning the war, in view of its enormous cost in financial and human terms. Their judgement may or may not be correct, but to the men under training in 1942,

Armstrong-Whitworth Whitley (*IWM*)

such criticisms would doubtless have seemed academic. Those arriving at 24 OTU at the beginning of June 1942 would be flying on their first bombing raids over Germany within a few weeks. For them it would simply be a question of survival, although it is doubtful whether they yet knew the odds against them. They would find that out later.

Bob had a few days leave after finishing the course at Shawbury. My mother wrote to him a few days after he reported at Honeybourne:

> . . . Well Bob, I wish you every success in your new flying course, and may God be with you in all that you do. This is my greatest wish, and I am looking forward to seeing you as soon as it is possible. I want you to give me a wings brooch as a keepsake. Don't think me too sentimental, but it is just a mother's feeling for a son that she loves dearly. I am going to try not to worry as I do not want in any way to upset you or your career. I only hope that we shall all be together again soon in our own homes. Dad and I will be celebrating our silver wedding next year I hope. Well Bob, once again I wish you well.

He sent her the brooch, mentioning the fact in a letter to Bill:

> I sent Mum a set of wings in brooch form as she said she'd like some. I should have thought of it before but as you should know I'm a thoughtless sort of cuss. Actually I had thought of it before but not at the right time, i.e. outside a jeweller's shop. I am always telling her not to worry, but that won't stop her. I had a letter from her a couple of days ago. It brought a lump to my throat, I must confess, unusual as that may seem. Poor Mum — she has had a hard life, and if I get out of this in one piece I am going to try and make her lot a happier one. Sorry for this sentiment but I am not exactly hardboiled yet.

In October 1983, Bill and I went and looked at what remains of Honeybourne. Most of the airfield has been returned to farmland, but a few yards of the main runway are still there. There are a few brick outbuildings in a decrepit state, but the hangers that housed the Whitleys are still intact.

Honeybourne
June 1942

. . . there are Whitleys here and they are clumsy cows. If a wing drops ten degrees, you need full aileron to pull it up. They are immensely stable, and you can sit them down from anything between two and ten feet up. Our kites have got Merlins with constant-speed airscrews. The latter are the first I've handled and are quite a revelation. The first circuits I did made me sweat with exertion; also when you put the wheels and flaps down they react in quite a different way to an Oxford. Whereas in an Oxford there is a tendency for the nose to drop, in a Whitley you have to shove like hell to keep it down.

We crew up later on in the course. I already have an Observer, a W/Op AG and a rear gunner. My Wopag is a naturalised American. He is only a little bloke about five feet high, maybe less. The AG is a Canadian. He calls me 'stretch'. Then the Observer is a Londoner, comes from Hackney. We are all sergeants but there are officers here as well.

One P/O Thompson has a Rover 14 which he drives like stink. He often takes us to Evesham. Last night be brought us back and let his dame drive. She had only started driving that weekend, and her average speed was about 60, cornering at 40. She didn't seem to realise the speed she was going. However she got us back which is better than walking, as Jock Greig and I did the previous night. We were both more or less drunk and we had about half a dozen sleeps on the way by the side of the road. There were some posts on the pavement and I swung my legs over them quite easily. When Jock tried it his other leg bent at the knee and he just slid down the pole to the ground. I go all hot in the neck when I think about the things we did that night.

Evesham is like a small edition of Stratford-upon-Avon with much the same facilities for amusement of Air Crews. You can guess what they are. The country is much the same as Kent and there is an abundance of orchards, all kinds of fruit, apples, pears, etc. They are not yet all ripe of course.

But the weather in June 1942 was gloriously hot, and the fruit on the trees soon ripened. Towards the end of the month Bob wrote to Mother:

You know this country is renowned for its fruit. Well I have had more strawberries, cherries, etc. than ever before in the last week. Cherries cost 1/6p a pound, and strawberries about the same. How are you fixed for this sort of thing in London? Just let me know and I will find a way of sending some home.

We are having quite a good time down here considering the very limited facilities. The country is very lovely, and we do quite a lot of walking. We got a lift into Broadway (from which the Broadway of New York is named). There was an elderly man and a stout old woman in the car and they invited us in for a cup of tea. (I was with Alec Combe, another pilot.) Their house was really beautiful, a genuine old English home and the garden was in keeping with a big lawn, rose garden, fish pond, etc. But, oh boy, didn't the old girl let you know it. She was a first-class snob, continually prattling about how she liked to entertain the boys, and the good work she was doing down in the village. The tone she used indicated that we had been hobnobbing with the élite. However we imbibed their tea, smoked their cigarettes and ate their cherries and were none the worse for it. One thing the old dame was sore about was that she only had two maids instead of four. Actually the house would have needed half a dozen servants to look after it but she was such a confounded snob, and bore, that I had no sympathy for her.

Broadway is a typical old Cotswold village with white stone houses and the sprinkling of antique shops. In Willersley which is nearer but somewhat smaller, there is an old guest house where we can go in the evenings and get supper. After which we repair to the New Inn which belies its name, and quaff a modest pint or two in the company of local farmers, listening to their amusing accents between games of darts.

Other pastimes are 'Pipe the floozie' or 'Hunt the village maiden'. This however is in the background as there are no village maidens worth hunting. Another one is 'Find the glim'. In this case you go up to a girl with an unlighted fag in your mouth and ask for a light. It never fails. They just shove a box of matches in your hand and make a strategic withdrawal into the nearest house. As they are all more or less related in the village this presents no real difficulties, your home is mine sort of thing. I have accumulated some half dozen boxes of matches in this manner. Don't let this give you a bad impression though. I'm still the pure innocent lad that left home 19 months ago.

Very few of the letters that Bob wrote to our father still exist. In June The March of Time sent him to South Africa to make a film:

Dear Dad

How are things going with you out in Africa? Everything in the bag by now I hope . . . As you see we are getting on in our training. As Davy Keenan my W/Op says, 'It won't be long now.' I think I told you about Davie. He stands about 4'8" in his boots. In fact when the canteen car comes along, the woman chucks him a hefty great thick sandwich and tells him to stand on it to reach the counter. He more than makes up for his lack of height with a constant stream of wit. He is an American by birth, but English by naturalization — used to own a chain of wine stores in London, and lost them all in the Blitz. We

Mother writing a letter in 1942

had a 48 hr pass some few days ago. I took a Canadian home, a chap by the name of Bob Weese. He is my tail gunner actually. While we were in town we went into an Italian restaurant for dinner. We had to wait a long time, so Bob Weese fished out some canned stuff, cheese and French mustard, asked for some bread and we got down to it. It shook the waitress quite a lot when she came along.

Robert Allen Weese had been sent to England a year earlier by the Royal Canadian Airforce. He was only eighteen years old when he embarked. Ten days before he had married a local girl, Marjorie, whom he had known for about six months. She was seventeen. They came from the small town of Belleville, Ontario. Bob, who was known as Allen by his wife and family, was the youngest of six children. As a child he was very quick to learn but disliked school. He could drive a car at the age of eleven, and used to help his elder brother Blake, who had a Saturday job moving sand, by driving a second delivery truck. My brother Bill remembers him as being 'dark haired and very

Fred Dupré.   David Keenan.   Bob Weese.
Bob Hodgson.   Stan Farley

handsome, very pleasant but rather temperamental and wild'. He disliked being pushed around, particularly by the Military Police. When the crew reached their operational squadron, he used to wear a white shirt with blue spots, and a red bow tie with his uniform as a protest.

Bob's crew was completed by another Canadian, Fred Dupré. Fred was quite the opposite of Bob Weese. At the age of 34 he was the oldest of the crew, and his experience and maturity must have been a steadying influence on them. He had worked as a radio operator in the goldfields of the North West Territory in the 'thirties, and could do morse at a collosal speed. He was about five feet nine tall, and was fast losing his hair. He was a charming avuncular man who had come across to serve in Bomber Command because 'the job had to be done'. He was married with two sons and had wanted to be a pilot himself, but was too old to be considered and had settled for Bomb Aimer/Observer. One other ability that impressed my brothers was his incredible capacity for whisky, which he seemed to be able to down without noticing it — an ability no doubt learnt in his gold mining days.

Both Fred Dupré and Bob Weese used to stay with us whenever they had leave. Our house became their English home, and they were very well liked by all the family.

The navigator mentioned in the letter was a tall dark-haired man called Stan Farley, who was nicknamed 'Chunkers'. He was very intelligent and was the same age as Bob. He was one of three children brought up in poverty living in the Mile End Road. His father was a van driver, and was constantly out of work. He had a young brother who had been killed when he fell out of a window of the flat they were living in when he was three years old. The third child was his sister Lillian who was six years younger than Stan. When she was born the family moved to Barking in Essex, where Stan, encouraged by his mother, began to do very well at school. At eleven he matriculated, and won a fee-paid scholarship to Barking Abbey Grammar School. He was very determined to better himself and worked very hard. He was different from the local boys of the same age, being quiet — almost refined — and he did not speak with the same broad cockney accent. He was a good boxer, and won medals in competitions. He was also passionately interested in flying, and like Bob spent much of his time making model aeroplanes. When he left school he obtained a post with the local education authority, but when the war came, he joined the RAF as soon as he could. He wanted to fly.

Dave Keenan, Bob's diminutive Wireless Operator, was about twenty-five. He had married Elizabeth Logan in 1936, and they lived at Tadworth in Surrey. Bill recalled him as 'a very stable person, graceful and good looking'. He always wore fighter pilot's boots: most aircrew wore brown suede boots, but Davy had black boots, like jack boots.

Apart from a brief period in November, 1942, these four and Bob remained together as a crew for the whole of their service. The process of 'crewing up' was a rather haphazard process, but it seemed to work. At their Operational Training Units, the men would wander around, fly together, eat and drink together, and eventually choose whom they would like to fly with. The pilot, who was captain of the aircraft regardless of rank, was the central figure in the selection process. As time went on, Bob's crew developed enormous personal loyalty to each other, and a remarkable faith in their collective ability to face the inevitably terrifying risks.

★ ★ ★

The mixture of Canadians, Australians, and other men from the Commonwealth, clearly inspired Bob to some radical re-thinking as to what constituted a culinary delicacy:

> We are getting a lot of American canned food, spam and stuff. I put some gooseberry jam on some spam and it went down very well. The Canadians here even split their sausages open and put jam into them! Try it yourself and see how you like it.

At about this time Bob received a letter from Hugh Feast, which gave details of what they were doing.

> I heard from Hughie Feast the other day. As you know, he is up at Lossiemouth, and he finds it just as entrancing as when we were up there a year or so ago. I also had a letter from Jimmy and learned that Tubby Kitching, you remember him, is with him. All three of them are on Wellingtons. Hughie seems to have trouble with the engines cutting on him.
>   Bob Weese has been in hospital for a few days with swollen glands. He is now out and seems to be OK.

The letter was to Joan, and Bob Weese added a post-script:

> Hell, I'm still alive, but sometimes I wonder how because I've got your little brother for a skipper. He's pretty hot though, no fooling. The only trouble is I don't have much room in the tail with him in the kite 'cause he has to sit back so far on account of being so tall. But we git along. Back home I'd say 'so long' — but when in Rome do as the Romans do, so 'Cheerio'.

Bob finished the letter:

> Well that's inside gen Joannie, if a little exaggerated. A Whitley is 60 feet long.

Whatever worries Bob and his crew must have had, they hid them behind a blanket of humour and silence. Joan explained: 'They didn't discuss their feelings, I don't think they really wanted to talk about it. They kept that to themselves and among themselves.'
  Their first flights over enemy-held territory were only a few weeks away, and the training was in its final phase.

> I have finished the conversion course and am now in 'B' Flight. Here we do cross-countries, night and day. Charman and myself have been held up in night flying. The aircraft which were allotted to us went US damn near every time we flew. Trivial things like tail wheel shock-absorbers etc. I managed to get my last hour finished last night. In the end the compressor which supplies brake pressure went for a burton and Charman 'had it' for the rest of the night. Consequently we have

to fly again tonight, and as we were given the day off, it is a hell of a bind as we have to report at 21 hundred hours. I did intend to go straight to Stratford today to look up some old acquaintances. Also there was a dance last night in our mess. Naturally we couldn't participate in this as I have to get half-tight before I can dance (Dutch courage).

Things look pretty grim in Egypt don't they. That was quite a wheeze of Rommel's to wedge himself in between our minefields. Our own mines covered his flanks. The Russians are admitting repulses now, around Kharkov. I wonder whether there is going to be a reshuffle in the Cabinet, or will WC retain his old pals. Aw nuts! I can't bind on politics, but it does make you think.

Our mess is now full up with WAAFs who have taken the place of men waiters and cooks. At times, as you may imagine, things become quite funny. Someone swears with a WAAF just behind him and are his ears red!

On the night of 31 July twelve Whitleys set out from Honeybourne to bomb the North German town of Dusseldorf. Only ten returned. Bob and his crew took-off at 2344, dropped their bomb-load at 0250 hrs and landed back at base just after dawn at 0617 hrs. Their training was over. To survive their early operations, they would have to be very vigilant, and very lucky. Inexperience seems to have been the main cause of the high incidence of loss among aircrews. If you survived your first dozen or so flights, you had a better chance of finishing your tour of thirty.

Later on when my father, who had been an airman in the First World War, met Bob's crew, he gave them all a stern lecture about what they must do in an emergency situation. He had a high regard for their strong loyalty to each other, but was worried that this might make them slow to abandon the aircraft if ordered to do so. He told them that they must obey Bob's instructions immediately since their own lives, and possibly Bob's, depended on it. He was very concerned about all of them.

Chapter Five
'Ditcher'

In August 1942, Bob was sent on detachment to RAF St Eval in Cornwall, a Coastal Command Station. At that time St Eval was commanded by Wing Commander Pickard who had become famous as the pilot of a Wellington bomber featured in the documentary film *Target for Tonight*. New crews were often used on anti-submarine patrols, first to gain operational experience, and secondly because Bomber Command did not want to release more experienced men on duties they felt to be peripheral to their main task. For Harris there was only one objective to be seriously considered, and that was winning the war by bombing Germany. The station records for St Eval did not list the crews by name, so it is not possible to know how many anti-submarine patrols Bob and his crew went on. However, on 27 August, a number of Whitleys took off from St Eval at about six-thirty in the morning. One did not return.

Sgts. Mess,
RAF St Eval,
Cornwall.
2.9.42

Dear Bill,

I expect you've seen the postcard I sent to Les from the Scillies and you're probably wondering why, how, etc. The reason was thirty-five thousand bucks which I spent in seven minutes. Yes sir! One Whitley straight into Davy Jones — last Thursday.

We were coming back from patrol and about 2½ hrs from base, when all the oil went from the starboard motor. The old Merlin went for about half an hour in this condition and then seized solid. By this time I had come down low, 500 ft or so, as the clouds were right down. The other motor wouldn't hold her so out went the SOS and back went the boys to the ditching stations. I held her up for another five minutes and then stuck her down on the sea. We got the dingy out OK and the aircraft sank in seven minutes — not bad for a Whitley. We floated around for seven hours or more. During this time we heard or saw several aircraft and fired off Very lights. None of them saw us however. A basking shark had us worried. It tried to swallow our fluorescene tablet which is hung over the side and dyes the sea so that other aircraft can see us. We were afraid its fin would cut the rubber of our dinghy.

Front and back of the postcard
sent by Bob to Leslie from the
Scillies.

At any rate we were spotted in the end and an ML [Motor Launch] picked us up and took us to the Scillies. I had to wander round next morning with no boots or shoes. I managed to get some old flying boots however, and we went over to Trescoe with a 2nd Lieutenant from the ML where we got some grapes. We were told there were some banana trees there but we didn't see any.

Hello Bill dis is Bob Weese. How is you, we is fine & your brudder has a new name. I calls him 'Ditcher' now. Give my love to Joan and all that stuff. Yours till we ditch again, Bob Weese.

Later, when he was on leave, Bob told Bill that he had very nearly been drowned. When the Whitley had hit the sea, the impact had knocked him out.

When he came to he was still strapped in his seat and the water was up to his neck. He just managed to release himself in time.

From St Eval, Bob was sent to 10 OTU at Abingdon to await posting to his first Bomber Command Operational Squadron. At the beginning of September he was able to get some leave and came home for a few days. One evening, with Joan and Bill he went to a dance put on by the Home guard at the Livesey Memorial Hall in Lower Sydenham. Behind the blacked-out windows, a three-piece band played Glen Miller arrangements, and groups of people, some in uniform, danced or chatted. Bob was very shy with girls and considered himself (probably correctly) to be a poor dancer. Although he had had one or two girlfriends, he had never been seriously involved. Bill on the other hand was quite the opposite. He was tall, slim, very good looking, and much more at ease with the opposite sex. That night he had decided he was going to do his big brother a good turn and fix him up with a girl.

While Joan and Bob went on to the dance floor, Bill looked around to see if there was much in the way of a pretty girl or two. One young lady in particular stood out. She was tall, very attractive, with a halo of blonde hair that caught the light. 'She's the one for him,' he thought, and pointed her out when Joan and Bob returned. It must have been quite a surprise therefore, when a few minutes later, of her own volition, the pretty blonde took advantage of a ladies' excuse-me and asked Bob to dance.

Bea Couldry told me her version of the same event:

I went to this dance with my friend Doris and her boyfriend. I loved dancing, and in those days you really did have to know your steps: it wasn't jigging around and shrugging your shoulders like they do today. I saw this young couple dancing and I thought what a handsome couple they made. He was very tall and good looking, and she was beautiful with a mass of coppery brown hair — a wonderful colour. He wasn't a very good dancer. He was struggling to manipulate his feet into place on the floor. He was in uniform and was wearing his wings. They weren't terribly old looking wings, all grey and tatty, and I knew he hadn't been flying that long. I thought, well he's got the courage to go out there flying, and yet it took more courage for him to go on that floor and do those few steps, and I felt, 'Oh, how sad' — you know. I thought, 'Well, I'm going to give him a bit of confidence. I'm going to excuse him' — I liked him, you see.

His first words to me were 'I can't dance,' and of course I already knew that. I said, 'Oh, it doesn't matter.' He said, 'I hope I don't tread on your toes.' I said, 'That's all right. Don't worry about that.'

We finished the dance without any harm coming to me, and then he asked me if I would like a drink. The drink was a glass of orange squash at the counter because there was no bar. I said, 'What about your fiancée?' He said, 'Oh, that's my sister.' I was overjoyed. We tripped the light fantastic for the rest of the evening, and then he offered me a lift home. The lift turned out to be on the cross-bar of a bicycle through the blackout. It was lovely. He sang the serenade from the Student Prince, 'Overhead the moon is gleaming', at the top of his voice. It was sheer heaven, I'm sure no trip has ever been the same since. I was so happy. I'd been such a Monica up till then because all the girls used to talk about their boyfriends, and I used to think, soppy things, and even though I'd got myself engaged, I used to think. 'Oh, how can people go dithery all about a boy.' You know, I used to think it was stupid, absolutely stupid. I really did. That was of course

GPO Poster *c.* 1940, featuring Bea in her job as telephonist
(*British Telecom Showcase*)

until I met Bob, then I knew why they went soppy. I saw him on every leave from then on.

However, there was a problem. In the atmosphere of wartime Britain, relationships were often heightened by the proximity of danger, and the emotions of separation. Commitments were often made which in normal times would have been unlikely. Bea was already engaged, but to a man she did not love. Furthermore the situation was complicated by the fact that he was a prisoner of war, in the Middle East. Bea had been brought up in a very strict moral atmosphere by what she described as 'Victorian' parents. In spite of being extremely

Bea Couldrey

attractive, she had never had a deep relationship with a boy, and simply did not yet understand her own feelings. She told me:

> I really got engaged because everybody else was getting engaged. It was comfortable being engaged; it was nice to be attached to some one, to have letters and write letters back. I liked his Mum and Dad, and they consoled me and I consoled them that everything would be all right and Harry would be home. I was fond of him, and I was at the age to get really involved with someone, yet I just didn't feel that way. We had lots of mutual friends and I liked playing tennis and dancing, and then he was going away so we became engaged. But I never really loved him. People may pooh-pooh this in this day and age, but there's a real thing about loving a man differently from everyone else — a real special feeling and you can't put it into words. I knew the way Bob felt about me, even before he told me. I knew because we had that affinity — it's indescribable really.

But, since Bea was still engaged to Harry, she remained loyal to him, and felt she could only break the engagement when he came back. She tried to keep Bob slightly at a distance, to try not to hurt his feelings.

Chapter Six
Wickenby, 12 Squadron

In September Bob was posted to 12 Squadron, at Wickenby in Lincolnshire, close to Market Rasen. Wickenby was a new aerodrome, having been bulldozed out of farmland a few months before. It had been operational only from the beginning of September, flying Wellington 11s and 111s.

Monday 5th Oct. 1942

Dear Mum,

Just a line to let you know that everything is OK and to thank you for your parcel. It was a trifle battered when it got here, most of the biscuits were broken but the rest of the stuff was OK.

It was good to be able to speak to you the other night. As I told you, it was Bea who put me through. I know I'm a thoughless cuss in that respect and I'm sorry I haven't phoned you before now. However, now that I know that it puts your mind at rest I will endeavour to let you know more often that everything is OK.

I shall do one or two trips as second pilot before I do any more solo flips. I think that it is the most sensible idea — to go with more experienced pilots and get some knowledge of the whole thing. You see we just don't realise how the folks at home worry. I suppose ours is a dangerous job, but none of us who are actually doing it seems to look at it in that light. In fact I get more worried over landing at night than when I'm actually over the target. Most of us seem to look upon the whole thing as a sort of game, foxing Jerry, and you'd be surprised to know the extent we can do this. I suppose the Hun does the same over here only he doesn't look upon it as a game as much as we do. 'Nuff said.

We have settled down here pretty well, though we have as yet no means of getting out of the camp. I went out for the first time in two weeks last night. We went to the local village and drank most of their beer. I hope to get enough time to collect my bike soon, but we have very few occasions (in fact up to now none at all) when we can get out of camp in time to go anywhere.

The operational record book of 12 Squadron shows that Bob flew on a raid to Aaachen that very day, as Navigator to a Pilot Officer Fawden, and again on the 6th as Captain with his normal crew to Osnabruck. The only other trip recorded in October was on the 15th to Cologne.

Wellingtons (*IWM*)

Bob's 'keep the folks back home cheerful' style of letter-writing was never more in evidence than in his letters to Joan. He rarely discussed the dangers of flyings on ops with her, and only on one or two occasions with anyone else. Typical of this sanguine humour was his first letter to her from Wickenby:

Dear Joan,

How's my little ray of sunshine? 'Lor Blimey, dere I was, wondering where my next meal was comin' from an' I looks rahnd der corner and sees you.'

Well here we are at our winter residence, a brand new 'drome, well dispersed, bags of mud right in the middle of the woods. Harr, harr me gal, come into the woods!

We have a dinky little Nissen hut all to ourselves — No 5 crew does it again. We've put 'Semper in Excreta' on the door and pictures all over the wall. At present we are breaking in the stove and the pleasant smell of flying paint pervades the atmosphere.

Much to our disappointment there are no Stirlings and for the present we have to be content with Wimpeys. But in a few weeks we will convert to the best of all fours (we hope). Wimpeys aren't bad kites but after a Whitley they are all cockeyed, the throttle, pitch control etc. being on the left hand side. Like trying to write left-handed.

But within a few days he was to write another letter in much sadder vein:

Bob, Dave Keenan, and Wellington 'G' for George

> Sgts. Mess
> RAF Wickenby
> Lincs.
> 9.10.42.
>
> Dear Joan,
>   I had a bit of a shock today. I was in the Flight Office when I noticed an old crew list. On it was the name, Sgt Feast. There was a pen mark right through it. I checked up and found that it was Hughie, missing on his first operation. It must have happened about a month ago. I had a letter from Jimmy Taaffe saying that Hughie was on Stirlings, but he must have been mistaken. I wouldn't tell Mum about this if I were you. As far as I know Jimmy and Tubby are still going.

If the War had seemed a 'sort of game' up till then, I am quite sure that the game was over from the moment Bob realised the significance of the pencil line through the name of his great friend, the 'tall, fair, and not very handsome chap like myself. . . A great cricketer.' 12 Squadron records show that Hugh Feast was killed on his first operation — a raid on Bremen on the night of the 13 September.

Although quite a large number of young aircrew were lost on flights from their OT Units, it was during the first few weeks at front-line Bomber Command bases that the realisation of their own slim chances of survival became apparent. 'Tim' Timperley was a Sergeant Pilot who flew on many of the same raids as Bob, and went on to complete 49 Operations altogether, including a spell on Pathfinders. He and his crew made the discovery on the first day they arrived at their Bomber Squadron. Interviewed in 1984 he recalled:

We arrived at Waltham, which is just outside Grimsby, on a cold, wet and dreary November afternoon. It was almost dark and we were shown into a crew room before we were told what time to report next day. We were hanging around waiting, so I started looking through what was known as the Authorisation Book, which is the authority to fly an aircraft for any purpose, and is signed by the Flight Commander. I was flicking through this book and I noticed that one could trace the names of pilots and their crews for maybe five or ten operations. Then sooner or later, it seemed that everybody failed to return. You just couldn't find a crew that went right through the book. Combined with the weather and the environment, it was one of the few times I had a real sense of gloom.

Morale was kept up because most crews believed it would never happen to them. If a shell had your name on it, then that was that anyway. For the most part, when bombers were shot down, it happened in a black sky, and if it was seen at all by other bomber crews, perhaps if the victim was coned by searchlights, then it would look like a crashing toy. Usually planes simply vanished: 'nothing being heard after take off' was the terse phase used in the Operational Record Books. In air warfare, unlike land or sea, the bodies of their fallen comrades were seldom seen by the aircrews, and consequently death was distanced.

In any case, between flights for those who came back life could still be quite pleasant. There was the relief at having survived, the sense that they were doing a professional and dangerous job well, taking the fight to the enemy; there were comfortable quarters, comradeship, better pay than ground crews, and the feeling that the cause was right and just.

October 1942 was also the month that my brother Bill was called up. He had volunteered for aircrew a year earlier but had been put on deferred service. He had been given a little RAFVR badge to wear, 'so that he couldn't be called a coward.' He was sent to Torquay for his initial training. Bob wrote to him offering some pointed advice:

Dear Bill,
    I was pleased to hear from you at long last. I suppose you've been busy, what with blondes, brunettes, cock-eyed corporals, and dodging church parades. It does rather sound as if Torquay is different from Stratford when I was there. I believe it has changed pretty generally all over the country at ITWs. You get a longer course than we did, 10 weeks as against 6. I was actually at Stratford for 7 weeks. You are pretty lucky having dining rooms right in your billet. We had to march miles to get our meals. It is quite usual for such establishments to be keen on games, but they usually lack equipment.

Bob in a Wellington's Cockpit

You seem to have been having quite a time down there with the 'kife' as you so crudely put it. I think you are getting a little on the er. . . randy side shall we say. There were always rumours flying around Stratford that the cooks were putting bromide in our tea. I think they must have been putting celery juice in yours. You want to get cracking on dancing though, there's nothing to it.

We seem to be progressing pretty well in the Middle East. I certainly think that it has shaken Jerry and the Vichy-ites. But Germany hasn't been slow in getting organised. I hear they have landed airborne troops in Libya and occupied Vichy France. We can only hope that they have had to draw on their reserves from the Russian front. As for the post-war struggle, I think you are right. What are all the de-mobbed factory workers going to do, especially the women? Personally I've a good mind to stay in this racket until I see what's cooking.

We haven't been doing a great deal lately. A low-level cross-country which we did a week ago was quite good fun. I was pleased to find I could still fly in formation, not having done this since I was at Shawbury on Oxfords.

I've acquired quite a reputation on my bike ever since I pranged a couple of WAAF MT drivers who were riding two on one cycle. Since then I've narrowly escaped being run down by trucks about a dozen times. . . a sort of vendetta.

Bob flew on one operation in November, to Hamburg on the 9th. On the 17th he wrote home to Joan:

> The weather is certainly foul all right. We've had a lot of fog up here too. I had a letter from Bill. He seems to be doing OK with the local talent.
>
> It may interest you to know that I wrote off our old Wimpey 'G' George this morning. One motor cut when we had just taken-off. We couldn't lower the undercart or flaps, so I landed without wheels and flaps on the belly. Dupe was sitting on the floor and this disappeared in a shower of dirt. Bob Weese went head-over-heels down the fuselage. Nobody had any bones broken, but Dupe and Bob were shaken up a bit. The Wing Commander came rushing out and said: 'What's the matter. Don't you want it any more?' Rather a pity, as it was a good old kite.

A Court of Inquiry followed and Bob was reprimanded. The official accident report said:

> Port engine cut out at 500 ft. Landed on aerodrome with flaps and undercarriage retracted. Engine failure due to broken inlet valve stem on No. 1 cylinder, caused by tappet lock nut becoming loose and vibrating off. Pilot flapped. Could well have maintained height and made a normal landing.

In addition to the reprimand, Bob lost six months' seniority, and he was posted to another squadron within a week. His crew were split up. Bill remembered Bob's account of the event very clearly:

> At the inquiry he was asked, 'Sergeant, were you losing height?' Bob said to me, 'It was fascinating because there was only one person who could answer that truthfully, and that was me. All the others were engaged on the hydraulic pump and other things. In any event they wouldn't have known, since they couldn't see the flying instruments.' Bob said he wasn't losing height. He was maintaining height, but was unable to climb at all. On the other hand they were only at 500 feet, the one remaining engine was screaming away, the oil temperature was going up and the oil pressure was falling, and the question was whether they could possibly get round the circuit and get the wheels and flaps down to make a safe landing on the runway. The engine that had cut out supplied the hydraulic pressure to the wheels and flaps. The only other way they could be operated was by using the back-up hand pump. At least 250 strokes would be needed to lower the undercarriage and this would take several minutes. In addition to this his speed was

critically close to stalling, and anything other than a shallow turn would be very risky indeed. He decided not to take a chance. After all the lives of his crew were at stake. He put the Wellington down while he still could. He knew he could easily have said he was losing height and that would have been the end of it. He looked round at these people who were there to pass judgement on his actions, and he thought: 'Why the hell should I tell lies?' He would not compromise his integrity for an easy way out. He wasn't bitter about the result: he just thought it was ironic. He was a very cool person. He said: 'It just shows you doesn't it? No-one could possibly have known the answer but me — I told the truth and was punished for it. If I'd lied and said, 'Yes Sir, I was losing height,' even if I'd been losing fifty feet a minute, I would have been justified in putting her down on her belly, and I'd have been cleared.'

Bob was sent to Kirmington, another new airfield which had opened in October 1942. It was situated about twenty or so miles from Wickenby on the Grimsby to Scunthorpe Road. The reaction of his crew was remarkable and shows the deep felt loyalty and friendship that had built up. Dave Keenan wrote to him on behalf of the crew:

> RAF Wickenby,
> Tuesday 24th Nov. 1942

Dear Bob,

How are you progressing at your new Squadron? Please forgive my unenthusiastic send off, this morning, but I just hated to see you go from here. Had you been going on leave it would have been truly wonderful. But it spelt the end of a really grand team which we shall always remember as number five crew. This morning I was doing my D/I on a kite when the tannoy broadcast for Sgts Dupré, Farley, Weese, and myself to report to the Commanding Officer immediately. To me this sounded wonderful but after we had our interview it was a different story. The news we received was in the negative of what we desired. And he informed us that the Group will not post us with you, but will split us up completely as a crew. He also states that as we were reluctant to fly with Simmonds, he would watch his progress on solo, and that if he wasn't satisfactory he would give us F/O Stammers who is on his second tour of ops.

I'm afraid Bob, your virtue of being too damned truthful has been responsible for all this messy business. We asked the C/O how about your coming back, and his answer was no! Apparently he asked you if the plane was maintaining height, and your answer was yes! This one word 'yes' has made all the difference in the world to our future as a team. Gosh, Bob! Why did you have to be so silly. Whatever happens, Bob, you were and always will be a top-notch pilot no matter what those armchair critic's decision may be. We've flown on 12 ops with you, and many hours more including a successful ditching and belly landing due to ropey aircraft.

Good luck Bob, and do write soon as we are all very unhappy without you.

> Yours,
> Your very own crew,
> Sgt David Keenan

P.S. Bob, give me a straight course for one minute you old son of a gun.

The inexorable losses of aircraft and their aircrews throughout the autumn continued. Perhaps irrationally, the aircrews felt their survival depended on sticking together. They knew that luck would play an important part in whether they completed their tour. The pilot was of course the key figure, and confidence in him as a person as well as in his flying ability was paramout. This perhaps helps to explain the rebellious bitterness felt by Bob's crew. They would not accept the situation, and all but refused to fly with anyone else. A week after the previous letter Dave Keenan wrote again and described a very tense incident with the CO:

> Stan and I got truly soused at a dance on Thursday last, and I told the Wing Commander that I considered him unfit even for Tigermoths; also, I told Morton that he'd be leaving us real soon for the Group's rule was to post anyone who pranged a kite, and as he had pranged a Lanc the rule would be applicable to him. He just grinned superciliously and never said very much. Although he did have to admit you were a better pilot than he was. But he didn't have to tell me. I know it only too well.

On the day Bob was making his way to Kirmington, Bea wrote to him, not knowing that he had moved. He had obviously fallen in love with her, and as her letters indicate he didn't know quite how to handle it.

> Dear Bob,
> No you are quite wrong, I don't think you are an old soberside. If that was the case, I would not enjoy your company so much. Have you started to grow that moustache yet? I don't know whether I should like you with it or not. Tell Dupe that as he hasn't got a head of hair to be stroked we shall be able to stroke his moustache, that is if he hasn't shaved it off yet.
> I went to the Haymarket last Saturday to see the 'Doctor's Dilemma'. If you want a big sleep I advice you to go and see it. I guess it wasn't a bad show but it was inclined to be heavy. Being by Bernard Shaw we may have expected it to be the same. Vivien Leigh was a bore, over-dramatic — you know the old-fashioned type that falls on bended

Bob and Dave Keenan

knees when she cries. Yeah! We were nearly on bended knees in front of the manager asking for our money back halfway through the show.

Out into the Haymarket into the Hong Kong restaurant for some chicken noodles etc. Boy! did we 'stuff'. I was bilious on Sunday and have since learnt that they were not chicken noodles, which makes me feel pretty bad, what do you think? I can't find out whose noodles they were that we ate. Now I ask you, Bambi, how would you feel?

I am sorry you weren't in when I phoned, but that wasn't the only time, I phoned every night that week. Now what makes you think that you have upset the apple cart? If you had do you think I would have bothered to phone Joan, and ask her to give you a message, or even bother to phone you myself? Youse inclined to make one feel dat sad pussycat when you says things like dat!

Within a few days of his posting to Kirmington, Bob was given a few days' leave and took the opportunity to write to Bill to let him know how the family was getting on at home:

I arrived home to find the house full of woe. Nini with earache, David ditto, and Mum just up from bed after a week of flu. A couple of days later Madeline went hors-de-combat with flu and is still in bed. The first three are a little better now. Peter and Cackle have kept OK and are full of beans as usual. Les and Ian are OK and Allen as well. Here endeth the family troubles.

I've been posted to 150 Sq. at Kirmington, Lincs. Address as usual, Sgts Mess etc. At the moment I am without a crew, but they are to follow. This is why I have got leave so quickly — still flying Wimpeys Mk 111s.

Les broke his glassses and has seized on the chance to do a bit of lead swinging. Ian, by the way has been a little, in fact a great deal, on the difficult side. He didn't help Mum with any of his little tantrums. I haven't said anything to him as I most heartily detest the role of being the 'heavy brother'. Dad will straighten him out when he gets to hear of it. I must congratulate you on your effort of writing to Dad and enclose a photo of him as a consolation prize. He's getting to look quite stately, pipe and new suit — and he said he wasn't going to buy any out there.

Back at camp, 150 Squadron had been stood down. Thirteen of their Wellingtons were being tropicalised prior to being sent to the Middle East. At the same time men from 142 Squadron at Waltham started to arrive and together with the home echelon of 150 Squadron combined to form 166 Squadron.

I spent most of yesterday dozing. After tea I went to the bunk and after three unsuccessful attempts to light the fire, went to bed. I think my language should have set it going. I used up about three days' supply of wood, all to no avail. The stove is a most ridiculous affair, full of sliding doors, detachable plates and grills — a proper Heath Robinson outfit.

This morning I learned that I am to be provided with a new crew. I haven't met them yet but I've been told that they are all old-timers, which is a little consolation. But I would sooner have the boys back.

Bill was settling in at his ITW in Torquay. He had a quite different personality to Bob, being much more outgoing and forceful. He was academically brilliant at school and would undoubtedly have gone on to university had not the war intervened. In December he wrote to Bob:

Dear brother Bob,

I was pleased to hear from you again. Both Joan and Les have written to me since and they told me about your spot of bother over the crew. It seems an extraordinary thing to break up teams like that, and if it wasn't a mistake, it would be interesting to know what it is all about. Anyway I hope things pan out for you.

I also heard that you enjoyed your six days with the family in spite of the ailments. I was indeed pleased to hear that you were making progress with B. I think she's a wow in all its senses. Indeed it was I, with my unfailing good taste, who selected her as a suitable partner for you at a certain HG dance, moons upon moons back. I do hope that you continue to find favour etc., and that's quite sincere, brother. (You big lug!)

We had a little navi. Progress exam last Friday week, and I was surprised and bucked that I passed with over 90%. That was the first hurdle and now the plot really thickens. Our finals on January 19th consist of the whole works: signals, navi., met., theory of flight, engines, law and admin, hygiene, and God knows what besides. Everything hinges on the navi and other things are secondary. I guess and calculate that with some effort I should get by safely.

I've had a rather unfortunate spot of bother with the two other occupants of the room. We were fooling around before tea, and they both set on me and the little Welsh guy started to punch me in the face. Then I let fly at them both and disposed of them after a tussle. Feelings ran high and they are busy organising a vendetta agin me, which is a pity as life is normally very happy here. However we must expect these upheavals occasionally, and weather them.

Christmas approaches and I am rather pre-occupied with the concert which we are giving to the squadron. With a public schoolboy (Blundells, old chap!) I am giving a Western Bros. act with some quite witty poems and rude stories which we have concocted. [The Western Brothers were a popular music hall act in the 'thirties and 'forties who dressed in top hats and tails, wore monocles, and mocked the upper classes with comic songs.] There will be free beer and cigs going so we may possibly escape alive.

I am still taking my music of a Sunday evening at the Pavilion. I met a Czech there who could speak French and we had a natter in that tongue. Next he appeared with two dames from Paignton. Later he was posted but the dames turned up anyway. I am taking them both (at their expense naturally) this evening to see 'Gone with the Wind' which is showing here at the usual exorbitant prices. One dame is young and pretty, the other is not so young or pretty. Mine is the delicate task of sorting them out and I shall apply my efforts to that effect. They, or one of them has a rich aunt and they invite cadets to tea of a Sunday. I could use something like that.

At Kirmington the formation of Bob's new crew was not going along very smoothly and he continued his attempts to get his old crew posted from Wickenby. The crew, for their part still refused to accept what had been decreed, and kept in touch with the family in London. Bob wrote to Joan:

I was immensely pleased to hear that Louie had 'phoned you up. I haven't heard from them yet but the Wing Commander here is going

Bill Hodgson

to contact the squadron at Wickenby and see if he can get them posted here, as there has been a bit of a mix up already over my crew. One of them is AWOL and will be on a 'fizzer' when he gets back. Another member was absent for a couple of days but has turned up. He was on a 'fizzer' but got away with a rep.

I've just received a letter from Davy Keenan with a number of photographs enclosed of the crew. He is on leave at the moment as are the rest of the boys. They've got a good man for a new skipper for the time being but still want to get back to the old firm.

And just before Christmas they succeeded. Their persistence had paid off and all four of them were posted to Kirmington. On Christmas Day after she had fed the nine children who were still at home, Mother sat down and wrote to Bob:

Dec 25th 1942

Dear Robert,

Many thanks for your lovely card and letter. I was very pleased to hear from you, and am very glad that you have your crew again and imagine that you all had a merry time and trust you will all go on well together in the new year, and may we all be together next Christmas. Joan and I spent a few merry hours with Tom and Jim the Australians at Aunties. They made Bram* and I drink enough whisky to make us

Fred Dupré, Joan, and Bob Weese

squiffy and on top of this we had to walk home, but it was worth it, it was a lovely frosty night. We are having our Christmas turkey when you come home.

[*The aunt was my father's sister Dora; Bram was my Grandmother, and the two Australians were billeted admin. officers.]

Joan wrote an account of the same incident. To appreciate the full flavour of what she wrote, it should be realised that my mother only ever drank at weddings, funerals, and Christmas. Even then it was usually confined to a glass of sweet sherry, or port at the most. She was also very tied down by the large family and it was almost unknown for her to go out and enjoy herself. She usually rejected all attempts to get her out of the house. Joan's letter reads:

On Christmas Eve, Mum and I, yes Mum and I went out on the razzle. We bundled the kids up to bed and left Tosha [Leslie] in charge. We went first to Hamlet Road and had one drink, whisky and liqueur — imagine Mum drinking whisky. Then we started off for Auntie Dora's — we had to walk up Anerley Hill and all Mum would say was 'Oh gawd, I think that whisky has gone to my legs'. We had to run for the 49 bus but got on it quite safely — I was carrying 6 soup plates, a jug and six tumblers, a bottle of scent, cigarettes, cards and books; so you can imagine what a job I had with Mum on one arm as well. We arrived quite safely at Auntie's. I went up to the Spa but it was just closing time; I just met Eileen and Doff [Aunt Dora's children] with their two Australians Jim and Tom. We all walked back and sang carols on the door step.

Then they started their usual jokes and fun. Mum was drinking her second whisky and lime — and did she laugh! I've never seen her laugh so much. Then I went to help Auntie make some other sandwiches and there was a terrific noise going on. They had made Mum drink another whisky and stood over her while she did it singing 'I'm Dreaming of a White Christmas.' Oh dear. Then Tom started on Bram; she was getting very merry and very coy. We nearly had hysterics. Jim in the meantime was phoning his CO to tell him exactly what he thought of him. Unfortunately, or fortunately, he was out so they phoned some other fellows instead and got them out of bed. We all spoke to them and wished them a Happy Christmas, and after a little more frivolity Mum and I decided to go home. Eileen was so squiffy she was sick. Bram we left waltzing up and down the hall with Tom singing, 'I'm 22 today.' We got home at 1.45 a.m.

After descriptions of the family playing cards on Christmas Day, the presents, and other activities, a few pages later came the sort of tragic note that must have been ever-present at the time:

There is still no news of Harry — the ship was torpedoed in a storm about 4 days off Freemantle. It floated for two hours, but owing to the storm they couldn't launch the boats. They've had planes out searching for survivors, because there were 500 people on board. Isn't it terrible — Poor Doff is really broken up. There isn't much you can say to help anyone at a time like that. She said she'd had a very sweet letter from you.

Harry Larthe was cousin Dorothy's husband. He was first mate aboard the liner *Ceramic*. There were only two survivors from the torpedoed ship. Harry was not one of them.

Chapter Seven
January 1943: Comedy and Tragedy

Over the Christmas holiday period Fred Dupré was granted his commission, and in rank became the senior member of the crew, though Bob remained captain of the aircraft since he was the pilot. As an officer, 'Dupe' was not expected to mix socially with the other ranks, at least not on the camp. Bob wrote:

> Whilst its nice to have a representative in the Officers' Mess we shall certainly miss his old dial in our Mess. . . As for New Year's Eve, once again, as on Xmas Eve we had to aviate. I find it quite impossible to get sozzled nowadays, even with a whole evening in front of me, so I crawled into bed after a beer or two.

The strain was obviously to affect him. In the same letter he wrote:

> Poor Dorothy, I was terribly sorry to hear that Harry is missing. He was really a first rate chap and I'm sure everyone who knew him will miss him. It was quite a loss, 500 people, and I expect many other people are now mourning the loss of their sons, and relatives.

The juxtaposition of the tragic and comic continued with the next letter he received from Bill, written as it happens, on the same day, 2 January.

> I spent almost all my time at Xmas on the concert, and the Western Bros. act (we called it the Prune Bros.) went down very well, thanks largely to the nice timing and confidence we developed for months beforehand. We dressed up as comic-opera officers with monocles, enormous wings which I constructed with paint and a bit of wood, and we were complete with pukka caps and silk rings about 2" deep. We put the show on again on Xmas Day for the squadron dinner with new stories, then again at the CO's hotel on Sunday. Here the audience were all aged and mostly infirm and rather high hat, so that some of the more risqué jokes didn't take too well. There was a grand old boy with a beaver in one corner who saw the point every time and his lecherous giggles at least gave us some encouragement. There was a certain amount of beer etc. going, and with the Flt Sgt PTI walking round in silk panties during the panto, a good time was had by all.
>
> Last Monday, and the following evening we put on the act yet again at the Wing Concert in Torquay Town Hall. This time it was glamour all the way, with a grand piano and a mike. And although due to bad

amplification some of the stories misfired, the songs went down big. Sheer talent, Robert, sheer talent.

Thus most of my time was spent on keeping up the morale of others, but on Xmas Day I went along to the Wing dance at the town hall, and there in the bar and over the road at the 'Castle' much beer and spirits was consumed. I found a very affectionate young Irish girl surrounded by admirers, and plunging into the fray, carried her off to a nearby cliff top by sheer talent once again. She was only 5'1" but she knew many nice parlour tricks. I was even ten minutes late that night, so I must have been good, tis true I don't remember very clearly. Boxing Day, as I expected, she ditched me on a date, and so it was back on the spirits and then to the cinema.

This was just chicken feed, mere pot boiling. I got it rather badly over a nice (really nice believe it or not) young thing. I kept on the trail throughout the holiday, brought her along to see the concert etc., but still she eluded me. Culmination came when she snooped off with another guy from this flight on New Year's morning. My chagrin was immense and I had at least two brushes with strangers on the way back alone. However I've picked up the trail again (I'm very keen, see) and I now await developments for a date on Monday. But I guess that in general one can't have flirtations, let alone affairs, on such a short term thing as ITW. The nice girls are wise to it, and the not-so-wise simply expect to have it popped in and no questions asked. Even a high-powered wooer like me has a little self respect. . .

I hope your affair with Bea goes well still. You are in a rather unfortunate position, Bob. Having reached the age of discretion, you have to think these things over carefully. There's usually no solution to these 3-cornered affairs. Only time can sort them out. I don't want to talk down, Sergeant, but as a toad, I've been under the same harrow myself. Fortunately I was at a bouncing age then, and sustained only minor injuries which quickly healed.

The early part of January 1943 saw very little operational activity at Kirmington. The remnants of 150 Squadron were still stood down, and 166 Squadron was yet to be formed. Bob and his crew were given a week's leave. Bob, Dupe and Bob Weese spent it at our home. They returned to Kirmington on the 19th and settled in once again. On the 20th, Joan went to work as usual to her job as a secretary in the Sydenham Gas Works. There had not been much enemy activity in the skies over London for some considerable time. A few days before, on the 17th, two air raids, one at eight fifteen p.m. and the other at four thirty in the morning had broken the period of relative calm. On the 20th it was clear, brilliant and sunny, and no trouble was expected. There were no balloons in the sky, and it came as a complete surprise when a number of FW 190 fighter-bombers came in low over the rooftops. It was thought to be virtually impossible for German

School in Sangley Road, Catford (*Manor House Library*)

bombers to penetrate as far as London in broad daylight without being picked up by our defences somewhere. They seemed to be bent on terrorising the largely suburban population as they dropped their bombs indiscriminately, and machine-gunned people in the streets. One bomb, with a delayed explosive mechanism, went through the side of a school in Sangley Road Catford, and came to rest on the ground floor. About thirty of the children managed to scramble out of the downstairs windows and run for their lives across the playground in the few seconds before the bomb exploded. The others stood no chance. Thirty-eight children and six teachers were killed. Over sixty children and teachers were injured. It was the most dreadful incident of the entire war for the people of Lewisham.

The gas works where Joan sat eating her lunchtime sandwiches was about two miles away.

Wednesday's raid was a lousy one — it's a funny experience being dive-bombed and machine gunned. I was sitting at the telephone taking calls from the other centres when suddenly — whoosh — brr. brr. brr. — the plane roared down, below the level of the huts, practically shaving the grass — Bang!, up went the barrage balloon in smoke — whoosh, again down came the planes. They set No. 8 gas holder alight and

No. 8 Holder, Sydenham Gas Works. 20 January 1943 (*SEGAS*)

sprayed all and sundry with machine-gun bullets and cannon fire. I saw a couple of barrage balloons hit up Anerley way. They cut a seagull in half and it dropped on our milkman's head. I bet he wondered what was happening. They machine-gunned a train near Kent House station, the County School had a few windows broken, but luckily the boys were in the shelters. The school that was hit was in Sangley Road, Catford — poor little kids, they didn't stand a chance, the planes were over within seconds. There wasn't much real damage done apart from that, but it was so terrifying. Mum was very upset. Madeline was out and she got down behind a wall and hedge in Trewsbury Road with Mrs Evans. There were some kiddies injured in Maple Road, coming out of school.

Mum got all the kids behind the sofa in the sitting room. Nini and Carole were out in the street and David was up in bed — so you can imagine what she felt like.

Obviously, it must have been very worrying for any mother of young children to be in an air raid, but it is difficult to know just how frightening it actually was for most people. The Germans, and for that matter the High Command of the RAF, believed that the morale of the civilian population could be broken by the terror of being bombed. Joan however, regarded the experience with what seems at this distance in time to be remarkable coolness:

> It was only when the raids started that you realised you were actually
> at war, and even then I never felt fearful for my own safety. I can't
> remember being frightened. I just accepted what was happening. I
> remember wanting to go home to be with Mum and the children, but
> more in a protective way. You were worried but you weren't quivering
> in your shoes. When the Doodle-Bugs came down near the Gas
> Company, later on in the war, I heard them coming and knew they
> were going to fall somewhere near. I answered the telephones which
> were ringing instead of diving for cover immediately. I was in the
> sports pavilion, and I eventually took cover in the plunge bath. When
> it landed all the glass showered on top of me, but I wasn't really
> frightened by it. I used to feel sickened and distressed at some of the
> stories one heard, like when three girls were trapped in the basement
> of a house and could not be got out. The gas pipe had broken and the
> gas could not be cut off in time. The chief emotion was one of grief
> and protectiveness really.

The incident of the bomb that hit the Sangley Road School provoked
strong feelings of anger and bitterness, with stories printed in the local
paper describing the pilot of the German plane as deliberately
selecting the school as a target. The leader of the raid Captain
Schuman afterwards broadcast a message from Paris boasting that
every bomb had landed on its target. Bob read about the raid in the
papers before he received Joan's account and commented:

> It was a shocking thing about that school being bombed. I wouldn't
> have fancied the pilot's chances much if he had come down near there,
> not that I think he realised that it was a school he was bombing,
> everything happens so quickly in the air.

Bea also wrote to him following his short spell of leave. They had seen
a lot of each other during the week, but the situation between them
was clearly far from being resolved:

> So you enjoyed your leave. I'm so glad because I enjoyed it very much.
> Don't think that I am being conceited in any way Bob, by saying that
> several people have said that they have loved me, but I have got to write
> this as it is an opening to what I am about to say.
>   You see, in times gone by, Bob, I haven't really cared about how
> anybody felt about me, except Harry of course (this is going to be a
> bit awkward to explain, excuse writing please). Their feelings haven't
> worried me, for the simple reason I haven't even had a simple regard
> for them. (Oh, Gosh! How am I doing?) I have admired you from the
> very first time I saw you. Do you remember me telling you that I
> thought you were a very strong character? Well, I still think the same.

I am very sorry that I can't say the same for myself. Oh no Bob! its no good you trying to convince me that I am. I remember you once telling me that I ought not to be walking around, do you remember? It was the second evening that we went out together. Well, I'm beginning to wonder as to whether you are right. Why should I wonder? Well, I've got two of the greatest fellows on this earth in love with me, and if I am not careful one of them is going to be terribly hurt. Honest to God I don't want to hurt you — believe me, I like you far too much — and I wouldn't want to hurt Harry. He's out there and I know for a fact that I am life itself to him. He had never even taken a girl out before he met me, and he was then 21 years of age. How would he feel if I were to turn him down? I'm going to admit Bob, I'm too much of a coward to ever do it. At least I could never do it, that is if I should definitely change my mind. What I am trying to say is that I couldn't write and tell him, because if anything should happen to him, I would never forgive myself. Honestly Bob, he is a grand fellow, and I know that you would think the same if you met him.

Please, Bob, don't let me hurt you. You can help me, you know. Do you remember me asking you as to whether all the main events of ones life were planned from the day one was born. You said, 'Yes.' Well I too believe the same, e.g. if you are meant to marry a certain person you will in time.

Please help me to play the game with Harry, Bob, to treat him just as you or I would like to be treated. By this I mean if it will help you in any way to stop seeing me when you come home on leave, I shall understand. After all Bob, I am not the only girl in the British Isles. I know that there would be quite a few that would cherish your love and return same.

You once wrote to me and told me that you would never forget me, no matter what happened, that goes for me too. I couldn't forget you Bob, truthfully. You are the only fellow that I have been out with since I have known Harry. Do you remember bringing me home from the dance and asking me if I would go out with you, and I replied: 'I don't think I had better as it isn't the conventional thing to do, as I am engaged,' and you said: 'Please do, *make me happy*.' I have told you since that those words made me accept that invitation, but that wasn't so. It was because I was selfish that I didn't stop to think you would fall in love with me. I must be selfish, otherwise I would have thought of Harry and you. Why you? I knew that it wouldn't just stop at one evening. I want to play the game with you Bob, that is why I say that if you do not want to see me again, don't hesitate to tell me. Although I do want to see you again, if it is going to help both sides I think it would be just as well if we didn't. However it is for you to decide.

I hope I have explained myself clearly in this somewhat muddled letter. Write and let me know the reaction after reading it.

Goodnight and God bless you always,

Bea

PS Remember me to the boys, and please excuse my foul writing. I guess my nerves won't even let me write properly.

The next day she wrote again, on a letter card.

Dear Bob,

I couldn't go to sleep last night as I had something on my mind, and that 'something', concerned you and I. As there is that probability that you will write and say that you will not see me again, although I shall understand, I should like you to know just how I should feel about it. We have had some grand fun together, and I feel that we should be depriving ourselves of the pleasure which we have found when we have been in each other's company, pleasure, to which we are both entitled in this wretched world. So long as we can keep our friendship on a friendly basis, that is, as far as possible, I do not see any harm in continuing to see each other. You see, Bob, I don't want you to feel at some time in the future that you have wasted your time, and regret that you have spent any of your spare time with me. Above all I do not want your feelings to be hurt. That is why I said that if you feel you would like to make the break now, don't hesitate in telling me. Another thing, supposing you should meet a girl that you were keen about, and you took her home, I can't see any reason why we could not continue to enjoy each other's company, because, after all, I'm a friend of the family now. I don't really know as to whether I am writing the correct thing or not, but if I have written anything which is not to your liking, write and tell me so, because I am broad-shouldered as you already know. I do sincerely hope that we will be able to continue as we have been doing without any hitches. Only five more weeks to go, and you will be coming home again. It seems more like five years though, what say you?

Cheerio for the present Bob, and keep smiling,
Bea

They went on seeing each other.

Chapter Eight
166 Squadron — Operational

On 27 January 1943, the two home echelons of 150 and 142 Squadrons were finally merged to become 166 Squadron. The Squadron had the motto 'Tenacity', with the emblem of a bulldog. The aerodrome was built on farmland in 1942 close to the tiny village of Kirmington. Today it is the small but growing Humberside Airport, but in January 1943 it was a collection of scattered groups of wooden huts and hangars partly hidden by clumps of small trees, and with mud everywhere. It was piercingly cold, with cutting winds, grey skies, and persistant drizzle.

On 29 January, twelve Wellingtons of 166 Squadron flew out on the first sortie, to bomb the French port of L'Orient which was being used by the German as a naval base. The Operational Record Book records Bob as taking off at 1715 hrs and returning at 2135 hrs. The task was 'Gardening', the code name for mine-laying. One Wellington, piloted by W/O R.M. Gray failed to return. Bob wrote to Bill:

> There's not much news I can give you. We have got cracking again if you know what I mean. I asked the Flt Com. about a commission and he said he'd see. He's away on leave now so its hanging fire à ce moment. Dupe has one already, got it a month ago. Don't you think that Dad looks well browned off. Did you see all the socks he brought home! You can get all the gen. on the politics, etc. of South Africa now.

My father had returned home from South Africa after a three-week voyage on board a converted cargo ship.

Bill finished his course at Torquay and passed with 81%. He was given a few days leave and then had to return to await posting to an EFTS. At Kirmington, Bob was able to relax a little.

> I went to WAAF dance last Thursday. I took my mandolin and after a session in the local I went and helped the band out. I don't suppose anyone heard it as it has rather a soft tone and there was a sax, a fiddle and a piano all kicking up a hell of a din. I tried hard though. Yesterday, Stan, Davy, and I went for a 'ramble' in the afternoon with a WAAF Sgt in tow, or rather she had us in tow. We went through some woods and immediately we left the threshold of civilisation, nature overcame civilisation and Stan and I reverted to our simian

ancestors. With many loud cries and thumping of chests we chased all over the woods. Davy put on Peggy's hat and pretended to be a gremlin. Peggy, (the WAAF Sgt, quite a nice girl) entered into the spirit of the occasion and gave a passable imitation of a wood-nymph. If anyone had seen us we would have been certified on the spot. Stan fell into a ditch with a foot of water in it. That is Davy, Stan, and Peggy in that order with Davy underneath. To finish a crazy day some of us stayed up until one o'clock in the morning listening to gramophone records.

I went and saw the Group Captain a couple of days ago about this commission, and everything is still hunky dory. I still have to see the board, but I am definitely hopeful. As a rule, the Wing Co. told me that a recommendation from the station C/O is rarely turned down.

Bob was again operational on 9, 12, 13 and 18 of February, all mine-laying sorties. On the 13th he reported heavy flak and searchlight activity. On that day, one aircraft was lost in a collision with a Halifax from 158 Squadron over Langport in Somerset. Another was lost on the 18th. Two days earlier Bob had written:

My brush with the MPs [it's not clear over what incident] resulted in an admonishment. Just before I went in on the charge, the Wing Co. asked me into his office and asked me if I wanted a commission which I accepted. Two seconds later I was being admonished. Life is not without humour.

He flew one more operation that month, on the 26th, to Cologne. One aircraft was lost.

He had not been home since his leave in January, and so had not seen Bea at all. They attempted to try to untangle their relationship by writing to each other. He seems to have been very upset by one letter, and must have written back angrily. Bea replied:

Dear Bob,

Just a few hurried lines before I retire. First of all, thanks for your letter which I received this evening in answer to my letter card. I am now going to proceed in answering your letter which you wrote last Saturday and I received yesterday. You said that you occasionally lose your grip and sort of burst — bing! Well that's the sort of feeling I had before I wrote that letter card, and the bing was in the contents of the same.

You say that I may not think much of you if you went back on what you said. Well to be quite frank, I would be disappointed in you, as I do not think you are the type to say what you do not mean. However we will skip it. Bob, maybe I will appear to be a bit slow (but then who cares) but what is the definition of an eighteen-carat heel?

I have never been intoxicated.

You ask me to forget the letter that you wrote to me because you would like me to. Well Bob, I'm trying. We'll carry on in our happy-go-lucky way.

Now leaving that letter I will proceed to answer the letter which arrived today. You spoke of my feelings being hurt after reading your cynical remarks in your previous letter. Well, I did have my doubts as to whether they were meant to be cutting. How does it feel being sober, did you say? Well, future P/O Hodgson, I'll have you know that I have never been intoxicated.

A few days later she wrote again, but this time the tone of her letter was much less strained.

Yes it was good to hear your voice too, future P/O Hodgson. Why I can almost see you in that grand uniform, boy! I bet you will look the berries. Anyway, who cares really whether you wear a chic uniform — you will still be Bob to me and to everybody who knows you.

One effect of asking for a commission was that Bob was forced to postpone his leave until after he had been boarded.

15.3.43.

Dear Mum,

Something I was afraid of has happened. My leave has been cancelled for various reasons, the main one because of pressure of business. Naturally I'm a little cheesed at this. It appears that I now have to wait for my commission to come through and how long that will be I don't know, probably two or three weeks now. I shall try for a forty-eight in order to see Dad before he goes before the end of the month.

It was nice to get through to you once again and I expect Bea will put me through again before the end of the week when I tell her the bad news. It seems it was a good job I had those two days off after all. Still I suppose the longer you wait the better it will be to get home.

Bob was granted his 48 hour pass however, and this time he managed to meet Bill (who had come directly from Torquay), Leslie, Joan, and Bea for a meal in a Leicester Square restaurant. It was one of the few times he talked about operational flying. Bill recalled:

I remember two things about that evening. Bob had recently attacked Cologne, and I asked: 'What was the target?' And he said, 'Oh it was the workers' houses across the Rhine.' I asked him the classic question: 'How did you feel about that?' He said, 'Believe me, when you're over the target you don't think about anything else but yourself.' I also asked, 'Do you pray?' and he said, 'I do pray, yes.' Bob was essentially a reticent person, not really given to expressing his feelings, very much in the British tradition of understatement.

They all saw him off at King's Cross Station, and while they were waiting Bob produced his cigarette case which was made of brass. He was very proud of it, but nevertheless gave it to Leslie saying: 'It's a present, I want you to have it.' Leslie protested saying that he couldn't possibly take it, but Bob was insistent saying, 'Just in case anything happens to me I want you to keep it,' and pushed the case into Leslie's hand. The train pulled slowly out, and Bea ran along the platform kissing him.

The 'increase in business' that Bob referred to in his letter to Mother was the start of Bomber Command's main offensive against the Ruhr. Air Marshal Harris believed that if he could send enough bombers they could overwhelm the German defences and inflict devastating damage to her factories and civilian population. He still believed that the German people would not be able to withstand such a battering, and that they would soon be forced to sue for peace. By the beginning of 1943 the prospects for launching such attacks had improved. Radio and radar navigation aids had been brilliantly developed by our scientists and gave the aircrews a much better chance of finding their targets. The Pathfinder Force had been formed to lead the attacks and mark the targets with flares inspite of Air Marshal Harris's opposition to the idea. He had argued that such a force would be elitist, and would be bad for the morale of the ordinary squadrons. The sending of bombers closely grouped in a single stream had also reduced the casualty rate. Bomber streams were less easy to attack, as the ground radar which directed the German fighters could only guide a single aircraft to one target at a time.

Harris's real opportunity had come after the Casablanca Conference in January 1943, when Churchill, Roosevelt and the other Allies met to coordinate areas of responsibility and strategy for their armed forces. The American Air Force chiefs still believed that precision bombing in daylight was possible, and they thought that with their Flying Fortress they had a bomber that really was capable of defending itself and delivering its bomb load with great accuracy. They were convinced they could succeed where Bomber Command had failed. They would take no advice on this. They believed that area bombing was ineffective and wasteful.

The Chiefs of Staff issued what became known as the Casablanca Directive. This paid lip-service to American ideas, and drew up an order of priority for targets. Submarine yards and bases were top of the list, then came German aircraft bases, factories, and depots, followed by a list of strategically important targets such as ball-bearing factories, oil, rubber, and military transport. Following the conference, an Operational Committee of the Combined Air Chiefs drew up a plan that was intended to give substance to the Casablanca Directive. Precision bombing would be carried out by the USAAF in daylight and the RAF would bomb the surrounding industrial areas at night. This meant in effect that Harris could bomb virtually any of the industrial centres he felt was necessary, in the only way the forces at his disposal could — destroying whole areas. In February, the number of sorties flown by Bomber Command jumped from 2,500 in the previous month to over 5,000. It was the beginning of what the Official History of the Strategic Air Offensive called The Battle of the Ruhr.

On the night of 26 March, Bob flew one of seventeen Wellingtons that went to Duisburg. All returned safely.

At seventeen minutes to eight on the evening of the 29 March, Sergeant O.E. Collins' Wellington lifted into the rainy grey skies over Lincolnshire. He was the first of twelve Wellingtons from Kirmington to take-off heading for the industrial and munitions factories of the small town of Bochum, a few miles East of Essen. The eleven others followed within twenty minutes. Last to take-off was Bob's aircraft 'H'. It was a new Wellington Mk X that he had flown only once before, on the raid to Duisberg. Bochum was not the main Bomber Command target, as that dubious honour awaited the citizens of Berlin. There were nearly five hundred RAF bombers in the air that night. The squadron from Kirmington joined 156 others for their diversionary part of the plan.

Even forty years later, Sergeant 'Tim' Timperley, in another aircraft of that raid, recalled the raid clearly. It was his twenty-second birthday:

> Once we had left the main bomber stream, maybe forty or fifty miles on towards Bochum, I remember thinking that it was unusually quiet. There were no searchlights, no anti-aircraft gunfire, no fighters, not even any sign of the other bombers. Of course, one would not expect to see much of them anyway, except over the target against the searchlights and fires, but nevertheless one usually had some feeling, some clue that they were close by. On this raid I felt this great sense of loneliness, even at one stage to the extent of thinking that perhaps we had made some navigational error, or our timing was wrong, but when we finally saw the Pathfinder flares hanging over the target, I knew we had found the right place.

Bob and Bea   Tim Timperley

There was some flak over the target as we made our approach, and I remember thinking that this 'firework display' was Herman Goering's birthday present to me. We dropped our bombs, and as we turned out of the target area, I realised we had made a mistake and were heading in the wrong direction. I don't remember quite why this was, perhaps the navigator had given me the wrong course. I really don't know, but one thing I was sure about was that it was essential that we rejoined the bomber stream for the return journey. It was much too dangerous to fly on your own; you were too likely to be spotted on German radar, and easily picked off by a ground directed night fighter. The only way to get back on the right course was to fly in over the target once again and take the correct course out. In spite of the protestations of my crew I took the aircraft over the target once again. It was self-protection rather than pedantry. All this time I did not see any other aircraft. I still had this impression of an almost eery sense of loneliness. It was very unusual. It may have been that the stream was more spread out than normal because this was the first time that we had been to Bochum. Precise navigation at night was still very difficult. We arrived back at Kirmington a few hours later. It had been a very quiet trip.

Sergeant Timperley's Wellington landed at 0057 hrs, the third aircraft to return. He believes that he increased his chances of survival by

Sticking to the disciplined approach, doing the job properly, staying in the stream, and if one encountered a fighter, sticking to the rules of combat. In training, in a Wellington, we were taught to accept instructions from the rear gunner, in the case of a beam or quarter attack. We had to turn into the fighter just fractionally before we thought he was going to open fire, and because the pilot couldn't see behind him, he had to rely entirely on what he was being told. I only encountered three enemy fighters in the nearly fifty ops that I did, and only two of those fired at me before I lost them. Of course, sheer luck played a large part in it. If an ack-ack shell had your name on it, then you were lost anyway. I always felt that if I stuck to the parts over which I had control, then that was the most I could do, and I just kept my fingers crossed over the rest.

Tim Timperley felt that their morale was kept up in spite of the losses partly because when they returned from an operation they were the one who had survived, and partly because of a major difference between war in the air, and land and sea fighting:

There's a great difference between people not turning up in a crew room, and seeing, as people must have done in ground warfare, their immediate companions lying there either dead, or terribly mutilated. In aviation, if you saw somebody being shot down, you didn't see individual bodies; you weren't close enough. Very occasionally you did see people abandoning their aircraft, and their parachutes opening up, but it was always far away. You didn't let your imagination run riot. People just weren't there the next day.

At 0115 hrs Flight Sergeant M.L. Dewing's Wellington 111 landed, the last plane to get back. Two were missing. 166 Squadron's Operational Record Book reported:

Of twelve aircraft which took off to attack the target of BOCHUM, nine successfully located it and dropped 44 × 500lb GP bombs; 1500 × 4lb incendiaries; 120 4lb × incendiaries and 136 30lb incendiaries. 'V' abandoned the mission as the captain considered the weather too bad at base area. Weather conditions at base were bad at time of take-off, but weather over target area was good. 'D' was attacked by an Me 109 and damaged. Other enemy aircraft were sighted and moderate heavy flack was encountered. Searchlights were active. 'H' and 'L' failed to return, nothing being heard after taking off from base. This was quite a successful raid, in spite of stiff enemy opposition.

Chapter Nine
Missing

In the middle of the afternoon of the 30th of March, the doorbell of our house in Sydenham rang. My sister Madeline answered it. It was a telegram.

> I knew immediately what was in it. I didn't open it, I just gave it to Mother, who was coming down the stairs from her bedroom. She opened it, read it and sat down on the landing half way up the stairs. She started to weep and would not move off the landing.

The telegram read:

> REGRET TO INFORM YOU THAT YOUR SON SGT JAMES ROBERT ARTHUR HODGSON IS MISSING AS A RESULT OF OPERATIONS ON THE NIGHT 29/30 MARCH 1943 LETTER FOLLOWS STOP ANY FURTHER INFORMATION WILL BE FORWARDED TO YOU IMMEDIATELY =
> AERONAUTICS KIRMINGTON

Madeline immediately telephoned Joan at work.

> She just rang up and said, 'Bob's missing.' I must admit I sat down and had a good cry before I left the office. When I went home Mum was ironing, and still crying. I tried to get her to stop, to sit down and have a cup of tea and let me do it, but she just went on ironing saying, 'I must get this done today, I must get this done.' I told her that he was just missing, and that did not necessarily mean that he had been killed, but I think she was convinced then that he had been killed.

My father heard the news at his office — he had been sent the same telegram. When he came home he went upstairs and just shut himself in his bedroom and would not come out. Joan wrote to Bea and the following day she came along the road to see the family she met my father:

> I could see your Dad coming along the road, and there was nothing I could say. I just put my arms round him and we both wept. In a situation like that you can't start talking about the whys and the wherefores; it goes much further than that, it's too deep, too distressing; it's beyond words, the feelings and the emotions. Your Dad was very grieved. Then I went to see your Mum and she was at the sink washing up, and that was a very tearful time too.
>   The last time Bob was home on leave, he said to me, 'Oh, Bea, you'd never lose touch with my family, would you, if anything happened to

me?' And I wanted to throw my arms around him and say, 'Don't talk like that.' I should have told him how I felt, but I didn't, although I think he knew. But it's the way you're reared; it always stays with you, regardless of one's experiences, you never really alter. I never have lost touch. I was always in touch with your Mum when she was alive, and I've never lost touch with Joan. I regard Joan as a good friend; we've been through lots of waters together.

While Bob was listed as missing, there was still hope that he was alive. Bill wrote to Joan on 3 April:

After the initial shock of hearing about Bob, and the consequent pain is past, I am beginning to think that he has every chance of being a prisoner or even an escapee. I know old Bob's philosophy of flying, the Scilly ditching and that other forced landing for which he was caned, are typical. He's as steady as a rock and he'd never take a big chance.

If your information about baling out is not just surmise, then it means that a signal was received, probably for a bearing by wireless. This means that at least the aircraft wasn't blown up. But we mustn't building up false hopes; we can wait and endure till we hear. It's a comfort when you consider that they are as hardened an aircrew as you can find, not likely to do anything foolish.

For several months, almost till Christmas, my family clung to the hope that Bob and his crew were still alive somewhere. Then one Sunday afternoon my father took off his jacket, sat down in an armchair and went to sleep. Later, after he had gone out to meet some friends at a local club, my brother Allen went into the room and saw a letter lying on the floor. It had fallen out of my father's pocket. Allen picked it up and read it. It was dated 7 May, and was from the International Red Cross. It said:

The report that your son and his whole crew lost their lives on 29 March 1943 was sent to the International Red Cross Committee at Geneva in an official German statement. Further enquiries are being made about his death and place of burial, and you will be notified without delay when any information reaches the Air Ministry or ourselves.

My father had known for months, but had told nobody. Of all his seven sons, Bob had been the one he felt closest to. Bill, he thought, had far too much to say for himself, and with his sharp mind and strong will, he had always been too ready to take him on. Leslie was more silent, but no less forceful, and Ian was going through a teenage rebelliousness that made a smooth relationship difficult. The rest of us were very young, and so it was with Bob, with his qualities of gentleness and intelligence, that my father found a close father-son

Jimmy Hodgson and his film crew, *c.* 1947

relationship. Obviously he was deeply affected by his death, but he found the greatest difficulty in showing it. It was not in his make-up to express his inner feelings to others, except perhaps in an indirect way. For example, two years or so before, he had asked Bill which of the armed forces he intended to go into when the time came. When Bill told him he wanted to be a pilot he snorted and said with barbed accuracy. 'You won't get accepted, you're too damned skinny!' Since Bill was extremely conscious of being thin, he felt deeply wounded at this cutting remark; it was not until many years later that he realised that father knew what was probably going to happen to Bob, and found the idea of his second son taking the same risks too painful to contemplate.

Both my parents had strange dreams about Bob's death. My father dreamt that Bob had not been killed when the plane crashed, but had baled out and had taken refuge in a Dutch farmhouse. Some German soldiers had burst through the door, and as Bob drew a revolver to defend himself he was shot. He had this dream several times. My mother had a dream that she said occurred on the night Bob was killed. She saw him sitting in the cockpit of his aircraft surrounded by flames as it crashed. He spoke to her and told her that this was the end and that she must not be too upset, because he was going to be all right where he was going.

I mention these dreams simply because they occurred. Clearly my mother's dream gave her comfort at a time when she was deeply distressed. Although my father sometimes thought his dream might have shown the truth, he must have known in his heart that it was most unlikely. The German army did not usually shoot crashed aircrews; on the contrary there were a number of instances where they saved the lives of Allied airmen who were in great danger from angry civilians.

Bob, Davy Keenan, Stan Farley, Bob Weese, and Fred Dupré were buried in the Moskowa Municipal Cemetery, near Arnhem in Holland. One aspect of this that was puzzling was the date on the headstone of Bob's grave. The first photographs that were taken showed the date of death 1 April, but the International Red Cross and the Air Ministry had told us that it was 29 March — three days earlier. It was not until researching the film, forty years later, that the reason emerged.

Chapter Ten
1984: 22 May

Just before nine o'clock on the morning of 22 May 1984, I stood in the entrance of a small hotel a few kilometres to the north-west of Arnhem. I was waiting to be met by Major Willem Duyts of the Royal Netherlands Airforce, who was to take me to the place where Bob's plane had crashed. During the previous seven months I had spent some time researching the background in an attempt to establish what had happened, and I had been put in touch with the crash recovery department of the RNLAF. They had discovered that the plane had come down near the village of Schaarsbergen, close to the military airbase of Deelen. The Germans had used this airbase during the war as the centre for their night-fighter defences in north-west Europe. My visit had been arranged by Colonel Airie De Jong, Assistant Director of Defence Information of the RNLAF, who had been instrumental in tracing the details of all RAF aircrew who had come down in Holland. He had asked Mr Leo Swaaf, an Air War historian who lived near Arnhem, and Mr Gerry Zwanenburg Chief Recovery and Identification Officer of the RNLAF, to find out what they could.

In the previous months I had spent many hours in the Public Records Office at Kew, and had established that of the 487 bombers that had set out that night to Berlin and Bochum, 33 failed to return. This represents a loss rate of over 7%, far greater than was considered to be 'acceptable'. Of the twelve Wellingtons that flew from 166 Squadron at Kirmington that night, only four were left by the end of the following three months. Sergeant O. Collins and his crew went missing on the same night as Bob; on 8 April, Pilot Officer D.H.W. Morgan; on the 10th Sergeant P. Hall; on the 23rd May Flying Officer A.E. Steward; on 21 June Sergeant A. Burgess; on the 24th Pilot Officer R.E. Currie; and on 3 July Squadron Leader A. Cookson. All failed to return.

The official loss rate of Wellingtons flying on operations from Kirmington has been calculated at 4.7%. This figure gives a completely unrealistic picture of the situation. It was worked out by comparing the number of operations flown with the number of aircraft lost. A much grimmer situation becomes apparent if the number of crews who flew Wellingtons are set against the losses. Between January 1943 when 166 Squadron was formed, and September that year when the Wellingtons were phased out, seventy crews were used. Of these, thirty-nine failed to return. Of the thirty-one that survived, some had completed their tour of thirty operations and were given six months 'rest' before being expected to do a second tour. Some went on to become Pathfinders, but most went on to face the same odds flying in Lancasters or other four-engined bombers. It is unlikely that many survived.

All of the young men who Bob mentioned in letters written when they were under training were killed. The names of Hugh Feast, Alf Kitching, Bob Wells, and Jimmy Taaffe are all recorded in the book of remembrance in the church of St Clement Danes in London.

By the end of the war, over 55,000 aircrew of Bomber Command and 78,000 men of the USAAF had lost their lives. At the time there was much criticism of both morality and the effectiveness of bombing operations, particularly because of the enormous cost and the exaggerated claims of success. No one now disputes that the huge destruction inflicted on German cities by 1945 made a significant contribution to winning the war. However, it is now quite clear that in spite of the bombing German industrial production *rose* throughout the war. This was largely due to the enormous under-capacity in the German economy at the start of the war, and to the resourcefulness of the German people in re-siting factories where they were difficult to hit. It is now a matter of history that it was the defeat of German troops on the ground in Russia, together with the post D-Day advance through Europe, that brought about the end of Hitler's Germany. Very few people now argue that Air Marshall Harris's view, that his bombers alone could have finished the War, can be substantiated. At best it can be said that our bombers were able to inflict considerable damage at a time when there was no other means, and that it kept alive the hopes of all those living under German occupation. Whether the achievements of the airmen of Bomber Command can be justified in terms of the loss of so many of our finest young men is clearly open to question. Any criticism, however, has to be separated from the extraordinary record of courage and fortitude of the men who flew in the aircraft. Much of what one can read about the history of Bomber Command, and learn in conversation with the men who took part leaves one with nothing but admiration for their intelligence and strength of character. It is rather sad that these qualities now seem to have diminished with time, at least in their own minds. One ex-bomb aimer said to me:

For years I didn't think much about what we did. We had a job to do, and simply got on with it. But recently it's been on my mind quite a lot. They say we didn't do a great deal of damage. I know it was very difficult to hit the target, with the plane weaving around to avoid the flak. Most of my bombs probably fell in fields. I hope so. I don't like to think that I killed women and children.

In spite of this, his loyalty to 'Butch' Harris remained undiminished, although he thought the bombing of Dresden was quite unnecessary. Now, forty years on, his thoughts often went back to the men he had served with, and those who had not been as lucky as he had been on those dark nights over Europe.

My parents, of course, knew that Bob and his crew had been buried in the Moscowa Municipal Cemetery just north of Arnhem. After they war they went on the only continental holiday my mother could be persuaded to take. In Arnhem they met Riny Palm, a young Dutch girl. Riny had taken part in an official ceremony at the cemetery in 1948 with a party of Girl Guides, and had later gone back on her own. She read the names on the stones and wanted to know who these men were who had died fighting to free her country. She wanted to do something to show her gratitude and happiness at her new-found freedom, and her sadness that these young men had died, so she had written to my mother and asked whether she could look after Bob's grave. She has gone on caring for it ever since.

Riny Palm at the grave

Riny Palm was with Major Duyts when they drove up to my hotel. Colonel De Jong had contacted her and arranged for her to come with us to the crash site, which she had never seen. Major Duyts, an energetic and pleasant man, told me that they thought they had found a witness to the crash, and that he would translate, since she was an elderly lady who spoke no English. First of all, however, we had to go to the airbase at Deelen to meet Leo Swaaf, the local historian, who had been researching details of what had happened. As we drove to Deelen along a country round we went past some houses on the left hand side and Duyts slowed the car.

'Your brother's plane crashed in the back garden of those houses over there,' he informed me. It was the first shock. Somehow I had always imagined that they had come down in some remote place, and that they had not been found for some time. Yet here I was being told that it was just over there, close to the road and just behind that house. 'We'll come back this afternoon. We still have to confirm that the lady can see you.' The car accelerated on past some woods. It was on the edge of a National Park, and it seemed to me to be somehow incongruous that they had died in such a beautiful place. It had rained heavily the day before, and the dampness intensified the colours as the morning sunlight shone through the silver birch and beech trees that lined the road.

At the airbase I met Leo Zwaaf, who told me that there were several people who remembered going to see the crash on the following day, but only one person who had actually seen it happen. This was Mrs Van Hunen, the elderly lady that Willem Duyts had referred to. She had lived in the house behind which the plane had crashed.

I showed them all some photographs of Bob and his crew, and then read out some of his letters. They were very interested: they knew the names of so many airmen who had been killed in Holland, but not much else about them.

Later, as we went to have lunch in the Officers' Mess, we drove through the airfield and Major Duyts pointed out the Station Headquarters and various other buildings. They had been constructed using forced labour during the war to make Deelen into the biggest German airbase in occupied Europe. In order to try to disguise them from the air, the buildings had been made in the style of farmhouses, 'But,' Major Duyts told me with a smile, 'the Germans had built them to look like German farmhouses, not Dutch.'

At three o'clock, we pulled up off the road opposite the group of houses we had passed earlier. Each was well separated from the next, well back from the road with extensive rear gardens backing onto woods. They were built in the traditional Dutch style with high roofs, and were semi-detached. We were greeted at the front door by a tall grey-haired woman in her sixties: Mrs Van Hunen.

She had indeed seen an aircraft crashing that night, and remembered it vividly. She had just gone to bed at about eleven o'clock when she heard the sound of an aircraft flying very low. The sky became very bright — 'like daylight'. She was very frightened because she realised the light was from a burning plane, which she thought was going to crash on the house. She leapt out of bed and went to the window of the room at the front of the house. As she did so, the burning plane hurtled past her window not more than a few yards above — so close that it passed in between the front of the house and a line of trees bordering the road about thirty yards away. She screamed to her husband to take their young baby downstairs. Meanwhile, the plane, which must have been in a steep turn, came round in an arc and crashed in the rear garden of her house, only thirty yards away.

She discovered afterwards that a wing had clipped the roof of the house next door, and broken off. Petrol had poured down their stairs and hallway, but fortunately had not caught fire. Mrs Van Hunen had then rushed to her back room to look out of the window. She saw the wreckage burning fiercely. Ammunition started to go off. The crash was very close to the airfield at Deelen, and very soon the fire brigade from there arrived and attempted to put out the flames. In the end they gave up, and the wreck was left to burn itself out. The time and description of what happened (confirmed by captured German records) left no doubt that this was Bob's Wellington.

Very early the following morning, Mrs Van Hunen's sister, who lived next door, had looked out to see what had happened. The wreckage was completely burnt out, with little that remained of the aircraft recognisable. She could see four bodies. The Germans arrived shortly afterwards, removed them, and laid them alongside the wreck. They searched their pockets, and then went through the debris. Meanwhile, Mrs Van Hunen had gone into her back garden, and right at the end she found the fifth member of the crew lying face down on a bank. He had his parachute on, but it was unopened. Unlike the others he was not burnt; he seemed to have only a few scratches, but he was also dead. She said he was very tall and thin, with black hair that was long in the front. I showed her a photograph of the crew and she pointed to Bob, saying that it was him. (Stan Farley was also over six feet high with dark hair, but he was not in this particular photograph. It might also have been him. After forty years it is difficult to be certain.)

When the Germans saw that Mrs Van Hunen had found a body, she was ordered back into the house. After a search, the body was taken and laid alongside the others. The Germans were enlarging the airbase at that particular time. They had recruited local Dutch labour and forced them to work on the project. On the morning of the crash, groups of these workers were brought to the back of the house, and made to look at the remains of Bob and his crew as they lay alongside the wreckage of their plane. This public spectacle went on until midday, when the bodies were put into coffins and taken away.

Two days later, on 1 April they were handed over to the Dutch authorities at the Moscowa Municipal Cemetery. No information was given by the Germans about when they had crashed, or where they had come from. There were no doctor's certificates giving the cause of death, which was usual in such incidents. The Germans simply ordered them to be buried at once. The date of 1 April was thus put on their headstones, and it was only later that the International Red Cross added crosses with the correct date.

It has not been possible to discover why the Germans behaved like this, or who was responsible. The sound of RAF bombers going across Europe every night gave hope to those living under occupation, countering German propaganda which claimed that the British were virtually defeated. One can only speculate that they did not want heroes to be made of the airmen who had died. Perhaps they also felt the need to demonstrate what happened to those who opposed the Third Reich. As far as the local Dutch population was concerned however, they failed. The authorities at the cemetery buried Bob and his crew in the central avenue. The Germans did not know that this was the place of honour, where before the war only the most important were laid to rest. Dutch resistance fighters and RAF aircrews were put alongside each other, and in defiance of German orders, their graves were strewn with flowers every day.

After Mrs Van Hunen had told us what had happened, she showed us the exact spot where it had happened. It was next to a pine tree, a young sapling in 1943, but now seventy feet high. She remembered that her neighbour had been annoyed, because one of the engines landed on his newly sown vegetable garden.

She showed us a medallion that she had found in the wreckage. It was about an inch and a half in diameter, made of copper, and slightly curved, with small lugs on either side. It might have been sewn to a wrist strap, or nailed onto a piece of wood. On the front was a picture of St Joseph of Coperino, a seventeenth-century Catholic Saint who was the patron Saint of aviators. It was dated 1941 and probably belonged to Davy Keenan. It was not simply a good luck charm, but would have been a devotional item.

We left Mrs Van Hunen and went on to the cemetery, where Riny Palm placed some flowers on their graves. Only three of them are now buried there. In 1945, the two Canadians, Fred Dupré and Bob Weese were moved twenty miles away to the Canadian National Cemetery at Groesbeek. Whatever the reason for this it seems to me to have been an act that failed to understand the essential unity and comradeship of an aircrew. As a result Bob and Dave Keenan lie alongside each other, and, separated by the gap where the two Canadians had been, is the grave of Stan Farley.

Although Riny Palm has married and had a family, she has always found the time to look after the graves, and visit them on Bob's birthday and on the anniversary of the day when he was killed. The local people still scatter flowers on the graves of all those who lie in that central avenue.

Later, many of the remaining details were filled in. German records show that Bob's Wellington had been on its way to Bochum where it had been intercepted by a Messerschmitt 110 piloted by Oberst Werner Streib, Commanding Officer of the night-fighter squadron at Venlo, about twenty miles away. Streib had been one of the group of six pilots who had become the first night-fighter squadron. In 1940, he was the first pilot to shoot down an RAF bomber at night. He was responsible for many innovations, including the idea of the machine gun that shot at 45° upwards, so that bombers could be attacked more easily from below. He claimed 66 bombers before he was promoted to Inspector of Night-Fighters in 1944. He was awarded the Knights Cross with Oak Leaves and Swords, and went on to become a Brigadier General by the end of the war.

Sergeant Collins, the other pilot from 166 Squadron, and his crew, who went missing on that raid to Bochum, were lost on the way back. They went into the sea just after crossing the Dutch coast.

Relatives of the other men who went down with Bob were equally deeply affected. When the news of Stan Farley's death reached his family, they were trying to recover from a tragic event that had befallen them at the end of 1942: Stanley's mother had died of cancer, and they were still suffering from that shock. His sister Lillian was fourteen at the time of the crash. It is not hard to imagine the effect on her at such a vulnerable age. He was all that any young sister could have wished for in an elder brother: he was good-looking, tough, physically strong, and clever. Like many families brought up in the East End of London, their life had been very hard, with poverty and hunger always closeby. Stanley was their main hope that the future held something better. They were proud of his achievements, particularly of his becoming a navigator in the RAF, so his loss was a tremendous blow to them. His father was quite unable to cope with what had happened. He was particularly bitter because two letters arrived in the same post a month after Stanley had been reported missing. One letter confirmed his death, while the other informed them that he had been promoted to the rank of Pilot Officer. Shortly afterwards, the stress caused by these events became too much for them to bear, and the family broke up. The grief had made his father very unstable, so Lillian was sent away to live with an aunt. After the War he was able to come to terms with what had happened. He re-married and had two more sons, but he retained a bitter dislike for anything connected with the War for the rest of his life.

For the wives of the two Canadians, the period while their men were overseas was a desperately lonely time. They did not even have the consolation of seeing their husbands when they were given leave. The bombing and the food shortages that were part of everyday life in Great Britain were very unpleasant, but civilians felt that they were directly involved. The remoteness of living away from all this in Canada emphasised the unreality of what was happening in Europe. The strict censorship that was in operation meant that the servicemen were not even able to say where they were based.

Bob Weese had married his wife Mardie only ten days before he was posted overseas. He was in the Royal Canadian Airforce, and had joined Bomber Command when he arrived in England. Shortly before he went missing, he wrote to her saying that he thought he would be home on leave soon, since they had nearly completed their first tour of operations. Mardie was at her sister's house when she had a telephone call to say there was a telegram for her at home. Thinking it was the long awaited news of his coming home on leave she ran all the way back to her house. But the telegram contained the same bleak message as the four others sent out on 30 March 1943. Like the rest, she did not believe her husband had been killed. Even after the letter from the Red Cross arrived, she could not accept it. Eventually she did re-marry and have a family.

Louise Dupré brought up her two sons on her own.

For every one the sense of loss is permanent, and scarcely reduced by the passage of time. Forty years ago is yesterday, and the pain has not lessened.

There are names on war memorials, and there are medals and, of course, the memories of those who have lived on. But for the family there has never been consolation for the emptiness that is the loss of a son and brother.

These feelings were perhaps best summed up by Bea Couldrey. As she had promised, she kept in touch with my family. Her fiancé, Harry came back from the War, but it did not work out. They were not married. She now remembers the short time she knew Bob with a mixture of warmth and regret for what might have been:

> I loved Bob, and I wanted to hold on to him. I don't think I ever felt guilty about myself. I just didn't know what the outcome would be. I knew what I *hoped* it would be. I thought I would wait until the War was over, until Harry came back, and then I would tell him to his face. Today, I wish I had acted differently with Bob. I should have told him what I felt. I think Bob and I would have had a great future. We complemented each other. I am sure he would have made his mark.
>
> Underneath all that shyness there was a strong man, a deep thinking man. It was lovely to have known him.

Index

Abingdon 51
air raids:
London's first 10
April 1941, 'heaviest yet' 17
civilian reaction to 29
Airspeed Oxford 33

Bomber Command 41, 50 & loss rate 88
Bridgnorth 17, 20
Britain's RAF 14
British Screen News 14
Broadway 44
Burnaston 28
Butt, D 28
damage done/claimed in raids, report on 28, 41

Canadian National Cemetry 93
Cardington 17, 18
Casablanca Conference 79
Catford, bomb on school 71
'Chunkers': *see* Farley, Stan
Christmas 1942 67
Churchill, Sir Winston 29, 79
Coastal Command 50
Couldrey, Bea 52-4, 55, 62, 73-5, 77, 78, 83-4, 95
'crewing up' 47
Croydon 10
airport 10, 32

De Jong, Col Airie 87
Duisburg 80
'Dupe', the 5
Dupré, Fred (Dupe) 5, 46-7, 60, 61, 69, 70, 76, 86, 93
Dupré, Louise 95
Duyts, Major Willem 87, 90

Egypt 49
Elementary Flying Training School Burnaston, No. 16 28, 30-32
Elgin 26

Farley, Stan 47, 61, 86, 92
Feast, Hugh 17, 19, 20, 24, 37, 48, 57, 88

death confirmed 84
death, discrepancy in date of 92
entry to RAF 17
first Bomber Command posting 17
first flights, description of 30
first raid flown 40
grave of 89
Leslie, present to 79
Military Police, clash with 34
mine-laying sorties 77
missing 83
night-flying, progress in 39-40
no. 12 Squadron, with 55
Russia, his comments on the fighting there 35
Singapore, his correct estimation of events there 35
Squadron no. 166 76
starts flying 30
volunteered for RAF 17
Wings received 40
Hodgson, Carole 12, 20
Hodgson, (Caroline) Maud 12, 13, 64, 67-8
dream of Bob's death 86
life-style as child 12
telegram received from War Office 83

Groesbeek 93

Hamilton, Jock 34
Harris, Sir Arthur 41, 79, 88, 89
Hodgson, Alan (Allen) 12, 64
Hodgson, Anita 12, 64
Hodgson, Bill 10, 12, 14, 15-16, 51, 52, 58, 64, 76, 78, 84, 86
letter to Bob 32
Hodgson, Bob 5, 12
Bill, letter to on Bill's call-up 58
Christmas at Shawbury 34
Cologne, tells of attack on workers 78
crash-landing at Wickenby 60

Hodgson, James 13
dream of Bob's death 86
early years in film industry 14
post-war return to film-making 84
Red Cross, information from 84
relationship with Bob 84, 86
telegram received from War Office 83
war-time experience 14
Hodgson, David 12, 18 64
Hodgson, Dora (Bob's aunt) 67
Hodgson, Ian 12, 20, 64, 84
Hodgson, Joan 11, 51, 56, 67-8, 84
and raid on work place 70-72
hears Bob is missing 83
Hodgson, Leslie 10, 12, 14-15, 64, 78, 79, 84
Hodgson, Madeline 12
takes in War Office telegram 83
Hodgson, Peter 12, 64
Honeybourne 40, 42, 49

Initial Training Wing 24-9
International Red Cross 84, 86

Keenan, David 44, 61, 66, 86, 93
Kirmington 61, 64, 70, 76
Kitching, Alf (Tubby) (also spelt 'Kitchen' in some letters) 17, 20, 48, 57, 88

Larthe, Harry 69
Lea, Cpl 26
L'Orient 76
Lossiemouth 25, 26, 48
Loudwater 16

Maastricht 22
March of Time 14, 44
Moskowa Municipal Cemetery 86
Miles Magister 31

Oakwood Tea Gardens 27
Operational Training Units:
No. 10 51

No. 20 25
No. 24 40

Palm, Riny 89, 90, 93
Pickard, Wing Cdr 50
Portal, Sir Charles 8

RAF:
aircraft shortage 22
loss rate of aircraft 87-8
night-bombing, move to 23
Repton 31
Roosevelt, President Franklin D 79
Ruhr, The Battle of 80

St Eval 50
Scillies 50
Sedan 22
Shawbury 33
Strategic Air Offensive, The 7, 21
Streib, Oberst Werner 93
Swaaf, Leo 87, 90
Swanton Morley 24
Sydenham 10, 37

Taafe, Jimmy 34, 37, 57
Target for Tonight 50
Thousand Bomber raids 41
Timperley, 'Tim' 57
recalls raid on Duisburg 80-82
Trenchard, Lord 7, 21
Trenchard, Sir Hugh *see* Trenchard, Lord
'Tubby' *see* Kitchen, Alf

'Uncle Sam' 24

Van Hunen, Mrs 90, 91, 92

Warwick Trading 13
War Cabinet, Lord Trenchard's memorandum to 7
Weese, Bob 45, 48, 60, 61, 70, 86, 93
Weese, Mardie 94
Wells, Bob 19, 20, 24, 26, 88
Western Brothers, The 65, 69
Wickenby 55
Wilhelmshaven 22

Zwanenburg, Gerry 87

Appendix

The Hodgson Family on 21 February 1941 when the last child was born

Father:
'Jimmy' Hodgson (Age 50) Film Director and Cameraman with 'The March of Time'
Mother:
Maud (44) Formerly a negative cutter with Pathé Frères

Children:
Joan (21) Clerk at Sydenham Gas Works
Bob (20) RAF pilot under training — Formerly a Film Laboratory Technician
Bill (17) Student
Leslie (15) At School
Ian (12) twin At School
Madeline (12) twin At School
Alan (10) At School
David (4) twin (the author)

Peter (4) twin
Anita (14 months)
Carole born on this day.

Bob's friends in the RAF Under training:
Hubert Feast from Battersea, London
Alfred 'Tubby' Kitching from Herne Hill, London
Jimmy Taaffe from Malvern, Worcestershire

Bob Wells, Canadian
Crew:
Fred Dupré (34) the Observer/Bomb aimer
Stan Farley (22) from East London. Navigator
David Keenan (26) American, naturalised British. Wireless Operator
Bob Weese (19) Canadian. Rear Gunner.